POCAHONTAS AND CAPTAIN JOHN SMITH

POCAHONTAS

AND

CAPTAIN JOHN SMITH

The Story of The Virginia Colony

★

by MARIE LAWSON

Illustrated by WILLIAM SHARP

Landmark BOOKS

RANDOM HOUSE · NEW YORK

CONTENTS

POCAHONTAS AND CAPTAIN JOHN SMITH

RALEIGH'S DREAM

1

ONLY five years after Christopher Columbus had found the riches of the New World for Spain, there sailed from England a tiny vessel called the "Mathew." Aboard it was a crew of eighteen men.

The name of the "Mathew's" commander has come down in history as John Cabot, but it was, in reality, Giovanni Caboto, for like the great Columbus he had been born in Italy. Like Columbus, also, he was a seaman of great courage.

Across the stormy North Atlantic Cabot steered the little "Mathew" while the weeks lengthened into months. It was early spring when they left England; but not until June 24th did they sight land and found harborage at Cape Breton, an island east of what is now Canada.

Here the sea-weary men briefly rested. Here, too, they set up a rude staff, hacked from a tree trunk, and on it raised the banner of old England—the banner of Saint George, with its red cross on a white ground.

Then the "Mathew" traveled back across the long sea miles again. She must return home to England to report.

England was delighted with the news. Cabot was much honored, and again he sailed, never to return. However, his son, Sebastian, explored southward as far as Chesapeake Bay.

Thus did England claim her share of the New World.

Years later, in Canada, seamen under Jacques Cartier set up a tall, crude cross. On it was a shield carved roughly with the three *fleurs-de-lis* of the kingdom of France.

Thus the French claimed their share. As the years passed the flag of England was torn into ribbons

by the sea wind, and the tall cross and sh
France rotted into the earth.

/ Spain alone kept a firm grip in the New World.
She had conquered rich Mexico and Peru, Panama
and the West Indies.

Mirrored in the blue waters of the Caribbean Sea
were the treasure towns of Spain with stout walls and
high ramparts that bristled with guns. From these
towns, great Spanish galleons wallowed across the
Atlantic laden with silver bars and gems and gold.

England eyed those rich galleons with envy and
alarm. Spain was growing more powerful day by
day. It was time for action.

Out of England's harbors slipped English ships,
manned by courageous captains and daring crews.
Again and again some lumbering galleon was attacked on lonely seas, and Spanish treasure went
to English ports.

Then the English grew bolder. They assailed the
treasure towns, and lurked in the jungles to attack
the mule trains bearing treasure to the ports.

Guns roared on both land and sea, and Spain
voiced loud and long protests to England.

Even at that time, sounding above the angry
cries of Spain, even above the eternal thunder of
the guns, a quiet English voice was heard. It was

the voice of Sir Walter Raleigh, the favorite courtier of Queen Elizabeth.

Of all the reports brought home of the New World Raleigh had listened most eagerly to the stories of great trees and of a soil rich and deep. For he had an intense love of land.

Sir Walter Raleigh

He wanted to see, in the new country, homes for his countrymen. He hoped that some day there would be villages like those of England, with sturdy houses and shaded lanes, clustered about tall church towers.

Perhaps, beyond the towns, great farms with widely

rolling acres would grow green in the spring and golden ripe for the harvest in the autumn.

"I shall yet live to see it an English nation," were his words.

This was Raleigh's dream.

2

SIR WALTER RALEIGH was more than a dreamer, so he promptly set out to make his dream come true.

In April of the year 1584, with a license from Queen Elizabeth, Raleigh sent two small ships sailing westward. Their captains were Philip Amadas and Arthur Barlowe, and in time they reached what is now North Carolina.

Captain Barlowe brought back a written report, and a glowing one. It told of mighty forests and fertile soil, of abundant game and wild fruits, of "the goodliest and best fish in the world," and of the Indians, "gentle, loving and faithful."

Even the proud Queen Elizabeth was interested, and offered aid from the royal treasury for a new expedition. In gratitude and loyalty the new land was named in her honor—Virginia.

The following year Raleigh sent out seven ships, bearing over a hundred hopeful colonists. Sir Richard Grenville was in command of the fleet. A seasoned soldier, Ralph Lane, went as governor of the new colony on Roanoke Island in North Carolina.

As before, the Indians met the white men in friendliness, but there was soon trouble. Grenville got on ill with the red men. He thought a hatchet had been stolen and to punish the Indians he burned one of their villages.

Then Grenville sailed back to England for supplies, leaving behind him angry red men, and white men who were fearful of their Indian neighbors.

With the disappearance of the last white sail beyond the horizon, two dread diseases, homesickness and discontent, fell upon the colonists. They disliked the heavy task of felling trees and the dull work of planting corn. They spent more and more time listening to Indian tales of pearls and gold. They thought about the stories of some great water not far beyond the dark forest.

The old idea of Spain's wealth was still with them, and, too, that still older idea of a possible short route to the western sea, beyond which might rise the glittering towers of Cathay.

Whether the Indian misunderstood the white man's questions about great seas, and thought he merely meant some greater river or harbor, will never be known. It is unlikely, though, that the Indian understood those questions about pearls and gold.

The red man, so fascinated by the white man's stores, so eager to exchange his fine furs for glass beads or a tin dish from England, could hardly have known the value of gems or gold.

However, it is possible that the Indian was both wily and clever in his answers. Perhaps he wished to lure the white man farther away from his own peaceful villages.

At the end of ten months little had been done at the Roanoke settlement. Near the water's edge there were still only a scanty clearing, a fort, and a few cabins. Furthermore, no new supplies had come.

Then someone sighted a sail, and another and another, and men crowded the waterside. Those on the

beach were disappointed to learn that it was not Sir
Richard Grenville returning. Instead, it was that famous seaman, Sir Francis Drake, whom England
called "Admiral" and Spain called "pirate."

Drake had once more been in the Caribbean and
had merely stopped by to see how this new colony
was progressing. He wished to report to his good
friend, Raleigh.

Those twenty-three ships, laden with Spanish
treasure, caused so much discontent among the men
at Roanoke that they persuaded Drake to take them
home.

A few days after they had left, a ship arrived with
supplies sent by Raleigh. In another few weeks Sir
Richard Grenville brought a ship to the colony and
left fifteen men to hold the small deserted fort for
England.

But Raleigh was not discouraged. When he found
that Queen Elizabeth had lost interest, he dug deep
into his own private fortune. Two years later, he
sent another expedition under Governor John White.

It arrived at Roanoke in the heat of July with
eighty-nine men, seventeen women, and two small
children.

The new settlers found a few pitiful bones—human bones. The timbers of the fort and cabins had long since rotted, but the colonists started anew.

On August eighteenth, to Governor White's daughter, was born the first English child in America. She was named Virginia Dare.

Not long after, White sailed to England for supplies. Although he planned a quick return, he found England in a state of alarm. From royal palace to seaport taverns spread the terrible news—war with Spain.

Having had more than enough of English insult and robbery, Spain planned to conquer England forever with the greatest fleet in all history.

Governor White and his crew listened with sinking hearts to the news. They realized that it was now impossible for them to return to Virginia. No ship, however small, could leave England in this dread hour of her need.

Into the very harbors of England rolled the mighty Spanish Armada, a seemingly endless line of huge ships bristling with guns and crowded with armored fighting men.

In smaller, simpler ships the English sailed out to meet them, but those English ships were quicker, easier to handle, and—they were in familiar waters.

They knew the winds and tides. The light English vessels attacked from the rear, swift as hornets. Up and up they drove the Spaniards through the Channel and out into the stormy North Sea.

Those huge Spanish ships, overladen with sails and heavy cannon, reeled, floundered, and went down. Only a few reached Spain again. England was saved, and Spanish power was broken for all time.

Once again, after two long years, Governor White was free to sail for that neglected little colony across the wide Atlantic.

Complete silence greeted his arrival at Roanoke Island. There was no sign of human beings. Only one mark of the colony was found. Cut into the bark of a tree was the single word "Croatoan," the name of a neighboring island.

Again and again they shouted and listened for some answering cry. They wandered into the forest. Alarmed birds rose, and there was a crackling of broken brush, a rustle of fallen leaves, as the four-footed creatures of the woods fled before that shouting.

White begged the Captain to go to Croatoan, but storms arose and supplies were low.

So back to England went the ship, and White was

never to know the fate of his daughter or his grand-child.

Had the red men descended on that lonely settlement to kill? Or had they come in friendship and mercy, with food for starving folk? Had those desperate folk, seemingly deserted by the mother country, England, joined their fortunes with their red neighbors?

No one knows.

Years later, near the Cape Fear River, white colonists met Indians, bronzed, black-haired men, but many of them had the sea-gray eyes of Englishmen. This may be the secret held by that mysterious tree marked Croatoan.

This last failure would seem to end Raleigh's dream. His favor at court had waned. Soon after, his friend, Queen Elizabeth, was dead, and his fortune was gone.

But in those luckless Virginia settlements a tiny seed had been sown, not yet come to its growth. The memory of its planting remained in men's minds; it might yet rise above the earth, and come to its full flowering.

3

ON THE throne of England sat James 1st, only son of the beautiful but luckless Mary, Queen of Scots. James was a cold, proud man, and none too popular with his subjects.

To him went a group of men who were eager to form a company and to try once again a settlement in the new land of Virginia.

In that group were titled men of wealth, prosperous merchants, and men of experience. Outstanding

19

among them were a sun-bronzed seaman who had been to the New World, Bartholomew Gosnold by name, and Captain John Smith, a tall, brave soldier, lately home from the wars.

King James listened, but he was not much interested in New World colonies. He told his visitors that they need expect no money from the Crown to aid them. Nevertheless, he added, if "precious metals" should be found, the Crown would expect a share.

The group had his royal permission to go, and he would present a charter, giving it definite rights to a certain amount of land.

James was quite willing to give away something which had cost him nothing. Actually, the land was not his to give; Spain still claimed it; the red man owned it.

When the charter was drawn up for the new-founded "London Company," it was handsomely written with beautiful capital letters, and the royal seals were attached.

The charter was more than generous about land. What was then termed "Virginia" extended from the middle of South Carolina to the edges of New York.

In the belief that America was a narrow strip between oceans, a later and more lavish charter added that the new colony would stretch "from sea to sea."

Spanish spies quietly left the English court to report to Spain. Spain was annoyed, but delayed doing anything.

As for the Indian, that is another story. He knew nothing and cared less for royal charters dripping with seals. For centuries he was to fight the newcomers in his own way.

The London Company received its charter from King James in April, 1606, and by December one hundred and forty-three colonists were ready to sail. To carry them across the ocean, three small ships lay ready in the Thames River: the "Goodspeed," the "Discovery," and the "Susan Constant."

On the day of sailing, the dock was crowded with people come to bid farewell to some member of the family or to a friend. Coaches brought folk rich in furs and velvets who mingled with the more simply dressed wives of the laborers and the seamen.

The men of the London Company busily gave orders to the captains, and the captains shouted orders to their crews.

Then came a sudden hush. For the final ceremonies were about to start. A prayer for safety was followed by the reading of a poem, especially written for the occasion, by England's famous poet of the day, Michael Drayton.

Even in that poem, filled largely with poetic seafaring words, the old shadow of Spanish treasure persisted:

> *To get the pearl and gold,*
> *And ours to hold,*
> *Virginia,*
> *Earth's only Paradise.*

Now came the final orders. They were followed by the whine of ropes as the clumsy sails were lifted, and the clatter of chains as the heavy anchors left the mud of the Thames. There was a flutter of handkerchiefs and waving hands. Then the sails grew dimmer and dimmer.

The colonists ran into choppy waters rounding England into the broad reaches of the Atlantic and the little vessels rolled and plunged.

The ships of that day were far from comfortable. They were short-bodied and even when laden rode high out of the water. No one traveled at that time without fear of attack, and the high sides of the ship were needed for the mounting of a few cannon and to prevent easy boarding by an enemy. Because sea voyages were long, it was necessary to have broad, deep holds for food and other needful cargo.

By the time the colonists had reached the gray rollers of the Atlantic, every man aboard had had time to eye his fellow voyagers and to begin to make both friends and enemies.

In general, it was a goodly company, though its members were not the kind of men who could stand the hardships of the wilderness. Most of them were young and filled with the high spirit of new adventure, but there was only a handful of real laboring men accustomed to heavy toil. A great many travelers in that company bore after their names merely the proud word—"Gentleman."

It was the hope of many that a few days' journey from the coast might bring them to the elegant courts of India and Cathay. Certainly a gentleman would have to be well dressed to appear before the eastern kings! For this reason a tailor and a barber had been thoughtfully brought along.

And, ever mindful of Spanish treasure, there were several men skilled in the art of refining gold, a few jewelers, and even one whose profession was distilling delicate perfumes.

After the Atlantic storms had been left behind, the little vessels sailed the long route southward to the West Indies. Now there was little left to do but talk, and many were the interesting tales that were told. Wingfield, the oldest of the company, had been a soldier, as had George Percy. One of the greatest of captured Spanish galleons had been brought home by Captain Newport, who knew the coast of South America and the isles of the West Indies. Bartholomew Gosnold alone had much to say about North America. He had spent icy months in New England, bringing home a fine cargo of cedar wood, sassafras, and furs. It was he who had urged the London Company to try a new settlement in North America.

So, beating southward during the long days and nights, men talked of past adventures, but no one talked so much as did Captain John Smith. No man's experiences had been so varied as his own: none had so remarkable a record.

He had fought with the French against the Spanish, with the Archduke of Austria against the ferocious Turks. He had endured shipwreck, prisons, and slavery. He had fought pirates on the Barbary coast. Why, he had even been in remote Russia, whence he escaped with the aid of a woman.

Perhaps he did boast a bit. His listeners became bored. Sometimes they even became angry, for besides being boastful, he was a blunt man. He did not hesitate to voice his unfavorable opinion about some of his companions, especially arrogant Edward-Maria Wingfield and Captain Ratcliffe.

Captain John Smith

In addition to these personal quarrels, there was on board one small object which no man could keep from his mind, and which also caused trouble. This was the London Company's sealed and secret box containing the names of those chosen for the council in the new land.

Each man wondered, "Who has been chosen?

Will the men on the council be among my friends or my enemies?"

But the colonists had to wait. That box was not to be opened until they had landed on the soil of Virginia.

Exactly what Captain Smith said to lead some to believe that on landing he planned to kill all the councilors, defy England, and make himself King of Virginia, is not known. Whatever it was, Captain Newport decided that Smith would cause less trouble if he were kept by himself. When, for this reason, Smith was made a prisoner, there was the added disgrace of chains.

So, on April 26th, brave Captain Smith could only hobble to a small window for his first sight of Virginia, when there came echoing a joyful, long cry from the lookout—

"Land—Ho—Land!"

THE LOVELY LAND

4

TWO sharp capes jut out between the Atlantic and Chesapeake Bay. The colonists promptly named these for the young sons of King James—Cape Henry and Cape Charles.

At Cape Henry down went the anchors, over the sides the long boats were lowered, and many of the sea-weary men went ashore.

It must have been a trying day for energetic John Smith. Had he been free, he would beyond doubt have been in the first boat, the first man to spring ashore, the first to go exploring, and the first to write down all he saw.

But one George Percy went ashore, and he, too, was given to recording events. He wrote with delight of this lovely land, of its towering forests, its clear, swift-flowing brooks, its meadows starred with many colored flowers, of the fragrance of the air.

Against the dark forest there must have been the drifting snows of the dogwood, the flaming of the redbud.

The newcomers rejoiced to see creatures similar to those of old England; the deer, the shy fox, the scudding hare; to hear the scolding chatter of squirrels. There were, as well, "animals unknown." Perhaps they saw the pointed nose of the opossum, the black-masked face of the curious raccoon.

New birds were seen, too: the flashing fire of the cardinal, the brilliant blue of the handsome, screaming blue jay.

They came upon a great patch of wild strawberries —how wonderful a treat after the long months of dried fruits and meats and hard bread!

They found patches of cold ashes where the Indians had roasted oysters, but they found no villages. Although they did not see any red men, there is no doubt

that the red men were there, silent, hidden in the gloom of the forest, watching and waiting.

In the swift-falling darkness the colonists rowed back to the ships, full of talk, their recent squabbles forgotten in their enthusiasm for the new land.

They were barely on the ships when some man saw dark forms at the edge of the woods approaching on all fours, "like beares." Another moment and those bears were upright—Indians—and arrows came whistling.

A sailor fell heavily to the deck, pierced by two arrows; then Gabriel Archer, with wounds in both hands.

The Englishmen answered with a volley of gun-fire echoing sharply against the dark woods, over the black water; and the Indians were gone.

The wounded men were made as comfortable as could be with the crude methods of that day. Guards were posted to watch the shore and the river.

Now at last the great business of the day was to begin—the opening of that sealed box. This solemn duty had been entrusted to the three Captains—John Ratcliffe, Bartholomew Gosnold, and Christopher Newport.

The box was opened, and perhaps the three Captains smiled at each other and shook hands. All three of them had been selected as councilors. There were also George Kendall, John Martin, Edward-Maria Wingfield, Gabriel Archer as recorder, and —the seventh councilor—Captain John Smith.

Smiles faded. The Captains looked at each other, then back at the papers. It would not be too easy to explain to the London Company that even now one of their chosen councilors was restlessly rattling chains.

Well, they would give out the news and await the results. The news went through the ships like wild-fire. Smith had friends as well as enemies and immediately both sides gathered.

At last a compromise was reached. Smith should be freed, but not yet allowed upon the council.

Carefully, for a few days more, they explored the land. Then, leaving Cape Henry, they crossed Chesapeake Bay and sailed into a wide river that led inland. This they named the James, and up its wide waters they progressed slowly, looking for a likely place to settle.

They found one point they especially liked and named it Archer's Hope. But the water was too shallow near the shore, so on they sailed, every man alert for a good harborage.

Hour after hour some seaman sent the heavy lead

overboard to take soundings. Again and again came the discouraging sing-song "S-h-o-a-l wa—ter!"

Then, some eight miles farther on, came the long shout of the leadsman—of water, deep water—six fathoms!

Before them lay a peninsula, and into that deep water went the little ships, not to drag their anchors in treacherous river bottom, but to be moored safely to the stout trees at the land's edge.

Over the ships' sides the colonists fairly swarmed —eager and filled with energy. From the deep holds came the remaining food and other stores. There were rolls of canvas for temporary shelters, axes for the conquering of the forest, tools for building, cannon for a fort.

They paused in their breathless labors for a short meeting of the council. Edward-Maria Wingfield was chosen president.

Again, as the shadows lengthened, they stopped for divine service. At Robert Hunt's request a board had been nailed between two trees. On it he placed the Bible and the Book of Prayer. Over this rude altar was stretched a weather-beaten sail.

Every man from the three ships gathered around it and knelt with bared head, for despite their quarrels, and their flaring tempers, these were godly men, firm in their Christian faith.

Led by their loved chaplain, and mingling with the murmur of the river, rose the deep voices of men giving thanks for guidance on the stormy seas and for a safe landing.

THE UNFORTUNATE FEAST

5

THOUGH most of the men were not used to hard labor, they set to work to build homes and a protecting wall. The settlement was called Jamestown.

The forest echoed with the steady chop of hatchets, the crash of falling trees, the busy clink of hammers, the dull thud of mallets as the protecting palisade was set. Day after day men came laden from the river bank with burdens of cut reeds for the thatching of roofs. Clearings were made for corn planting.

In the midst of all this activity there suddenly appeared two Indians, tall men of great dignity, with high headdresses of many colors. The Englishmen, despite the differences of language, learned that the Indians were special messengers from the chief of the near-by village of Paspihae and that in a few days the chief himself was coming to visit. He would bring, among other things, a "fat deare" for a feast, and "make merry" with the new-come white neighbors.

The English were delighted. Surely this meant friendship, possible assistance, and probable peace.

When the chief arrived, he had with him about a hundred warriors. The English had not expected so many, nor had they expected to see the red men so fully armed with bows and arrows.

The chief signaled to the white men to lay aside their arms. Neither side wished to do so first, but at last the arms were laid down, still close at hand.

The deer smoked upon the fire, sending forth tempting odors; but it did not promise to be a "merry" feast.

The red men eyed with interest the growing fort, the palisade, the muskets. The white men eyed the arrows and bows. Despite attempts at friendliness, the air was tense.

Then some Indian picked up a white man's hatchet.

Perhaps he merely wished to look at it, but the owner jumped up and not only wrested it from his grasp, but struck the red guest.

Another red man dashed at the white man with a sharp wooden sword, and every Englishman seized his trusty musket. There were scowls, threatening gestures, mutterings, protests, and general uncertainty.

In a fury, the chief of Paspihae rose and, gathering his sullen warriors, departed into the forest.

The building of the fort was renewed with vigor, and many sentries were posted. The tiny settlement must have its sleepless watchers, but it is likely that no one slept too well.

When there were no other further signs of trouble, Captain Newport decided to go exploring up the James. With him in the longboat he took Captain John Smith and some twenty men. Up and up they sailed for some sixty miles, to a place where steep, low hills rose from the river, and the waters tumbled over huge boulders and tiny islands. Here they went ashore, and soon met Indians. The same questions were asked again—of some path or waterway westward, of some mighty sea beyond?

Gravely, with many signs, the Indians assured

them that a march of some five or six days would bring them beyond the forest, to a great sea.

The Englishmen listened with care. Now, indeed, they felt sure they were on the track of that greatest of discoveries—the pathway to the western ocean, beyond which lay the rich Orient.

However, they were unable to go on at that time, for Newport had to return to England. That tumbling water below the hills they confidently named the "Falls of the Farre West." Here today stands the capital of Virginia, Richmond, thousands of miles from that western sea.

Back down the river they sailed to Jamestown with this news, but the Jamestown men had more startling news to tell. Hardly had Newport gone up the river when the Indians of Paspihae had descended—some hundreds of yelling red men coming suddenly from the forest, terrifying in war paint. Arrows had fallen like hail. Only after hours of bitter fighting in which musket and cannon and even hatchets and knives were used, had the savage foe retreated.

One Englishman was dead. Many were wounded, among them four of the chosen council.

This was discouraging. They had hoped to trade with the red men for extra food, to live in peace.

By this time the fort and some cabins had been

completed, and the corn had come up well in the clearings.

There were suggestions that Smith return with Captain Newport to England for trial, but Smith refused. He would stand trial here. Here were his accusers, here were the men who knew him. The trial went in his favor—he took his place in the council.

Captain Newport departed for England to get fresh supplies. Ratcliffe and Gosnold remained as councilors.

With the departure of the ships it was a lonely little fort indeed. England seemed very far away. One small pinnace, left by Newport for exploring, rocked gently on the still river.

And now the full heat of the lowland summer was upon them, and the forest, with its dense undergrowth, was airless. Mosquitoes, bearing the germs of the dreaded malaria of the south, came in stinging swarms. The James grew muddy and sluggish, and as the heat increased, its waters were not only hard to swallow, but dangerous.

Men, staggering with the weakness of fever, hurled down axe or hoe after an hour's labor. There was hunger, too; the scanty stores were running low. They could have gotten some fish, but were too weary to try; some game, but they feared the lurking In-

dians in the forest. The Indians were very quiet these
days, but they brought no food for trade with the
white men. Now and again a solitary arrow came
flying from the forest.

Discomfort, homesickness, and illness brought
quarrels. Idleness left too much time for petty grievances and for suspicions.

Gentle Robert Hunt, the chaplain, moved here and
there, often stopping a quarrel, constantly urging
patience.

John Smith, growing daily more popular among
the men, tried to get them to work on more cabins for
their own comfort, more clearings for new plantings, more military drilling in case of Indian attack.
Some men would not agree to work—but more could
not.

Gradually suspicions grew into outright accusa-
tions. Edward-Maria Wingfield, from the first, had
made no secret of his dislike of the colony and its
discomforts. Now he was accused of a plot to make
off with the little pinnace and with a chosen few to
try to reach England.

By popular vote, he was deposed from the presi-
dency, and Ratcliffe put in his place. Ratcliffe had
never been well liked; he rapidly became less so.

Another councilor, George Kendall, was accused

of designs on the pinnace. He was tried, and by common consent shot.

George Percy, who had but a few months before written with such joy of the new land, faithfully continued his recording. But those first pages had been pages of high hopes and sunshine; these, of the summer, were gray pages shadowed by death. Day after day new entries were sadly added: deaths by fever, by Indian arrow, by causes unknown.

The worst blow was the loss of calm, competent Bartholomew Gosnold. For his burial squabbles were forgotten, and every man left in the wretchedly dwindling colony stood by to do him honor. They even used precious gunpowder when every cannon on the little fort was fired.

So wore on that terrible summer. If the days were bad, the nights were worse. Restless, feverish nights, filled with the perpetual whine of mosquitoes, the heavy, stifling heat, the terrible loneliness.

And yet, there was never enough quiet for real peace.

All around them were the many sounds of the wilderness, sounds which often brought a sleeping man awake in alarm.

Dry leaves rustled and twigs crackled as the wild creatures of the forest went on their wanderings. The repeated quivering cry of the screech owl often broke the forest stillness. Now and again the piercing scream of the panther was followed by the long, desolate howl of the wolf.

Every crackle and rustle might be the stealthy approach of the red man. The Englishmen could not even be sure of the wolf's howl or the owl's cry, for often in this manner did the Indian give signal to his fellows.

Each day they strained their eyes for the sight of a sail; turning, heartsick, from the river bank to find yet another man dead or dying.

By autumn less than fifty men remained alive.

6

THEN came autumn and cool winds blew upon the broad river. The fevers and sickness were gone. Each day the wild geese and ducks came winging southward, flock after flock. They settled in such quantities on the river that they could be easily taken. Once more the Indians came laden with sweet maize and tasty venison. The reason for this show of friendliness was not hard to figure out. Many white men were a threat to the Indian; this scant and weak handful was not.

All through that dreadful summer John Smith had done all that man could do to save the struggling colony. The men had come to look to him for guidance, and he, of all there, got on best with the Indians.

Still Christopher Newport did not return, and Smith knew there would have to be a goodly store of corn in the storehouse before the snows came.

So, in December, he left the broad James and sailed up a smaller river leading to Indian villages where he planned to trade for more corn. With him in the small shallop he took a handful of men.

The small river was the winding and muddy Chickahominy which was often made dangerous by dead and fallen tree trunks. Up and up they went, coming finally to a place where Smith dared not risk the little shallop further. Leaving his men to guard the boat he went on with only two Englishmen and two Indian guides.

In the gray weather the forest loomed dark and silent. They went on shore, and progressed on foot.

Suddenly the forest seemed to come alive. From behind trees stepped Indian after Indian with bows ready for shooting. The dread whistle of arrows came, and Smith's companions fell heavily to the sodden earth, killed by a dozen arrows.

Smith fired his musket twice and two red men fell sprawling. The Indians were still in awe of that noisy weapon of the white man's. They hesitated, and Smith, holding the musket before him, started walking backward. If only he could reach the shallop and his men!

Unfortunately, his good luck did not hold. Slipping on a patch of ice, he floundered into the stream. His musket fell into the water, and instantly strong hands were upon him. "Surely," he thought, "this is my last hour on earth."

But the Indians had no such idea. Smith dead was but one more dead Englishman. As a captive he would be a curiosity, a great sight for the Indian villages, many of which had never seen a white man.

From the beginning the red man had marveled at the paleness of the white man's skin—even more so at his beard.

Besides, the chief must decide.

Over the thin crust of snow the Indians, in their soft moccasins, stepped easily and lightly. Smith found the going hard in his water-soaked clothing and his heavy, sodden boots.

Soon they reached a village and the Captain was led before the chief, Opechancanough.

Smith had with him an ivory compass dial. If he could escape, that compass would be the thing he most desired to help guide him.

But with a courtly gesture he presented it to Opechancanough. The chief and his warriors stroked its satin-smooth surface—ivory was an unknown material; so, too, was glass. Clearly they could see the tiny needle move, but they could not touch it.

Smith, with the few Indian words he knew, tried to explain. Then, hoping for time, he talked more, and yet more.

Strangely enough, though the Indian was usually silent, he had a great respect for orations on special occasions. The longer they were the better he liked them.

From the compass Smith went on to speak of the roundness of the earth. Then, with gestures, he described the movements of the sun, the moon, the stars, and other heavenly bodies.

For a time the Indians listened politely. Perhaps then, they tired of the talk, and wished a change in entertainment, for of a sudden Smith was bound to a tree, and arrows were trained upon him. As he saw

Opechancanough raise his hand in signal, the Captain closed his eyes and waited for the arrows. None came—hands were untying the thongs on his wrists; he was led away for more food, and a warm shelter for rest and sleep.

By dawn they were on the march again. Other villages must see this tall Englishman with his fair skin, his fine beard, his talk of things unknown.

Village after village they visited, and Smith fared well. He was brought venison, turkey and other game, and loaves of the sweet white Indian corn The Indian squaws eyed him when they thought he was not looking. Shy children gathered to touch his face, his hands, his beard.

Farther and farther they were going from Jamestown. Smith, ever on the alert, tried to take note of each dim trail, each wandering stream.

"Where," he asked at last, "are we going?"

"To see the chief," was the reply.

"But I have seen many chiefs," said Smith.

"Yes, but they were only minor chieftains," the warrior answered. "Soon you will see the great chief, ruler of them all, monarch of all the lands and all the rivers: Powhatan—at Werowocomoco, on the Pamunkey River."

Coming from the dark forest, Smith saw the gleam of water. On a steep bluff above it were many huts, with smoke rising. They were soon there.

One larger shelter stood apart, and into this Smith was led to see, for the first time, the mighty chief of chiefs, the all-powerful Powhatan. He sat on a raised platform—a sort of crude throne. Back of him stood armed warriors. At his feet clustered women and girls.

Powhatan was very tall, his face lined and grim. His great arms were weighted with copper bracelets. Around his neck hung many strings of what appeared to be pearls. And about him there fell a massive robe, made of raccoon skins, with "all the tails hanging by."

The shrewd Captain Smith failed to note the lesson of that garment. Its strong black-and-buff tails would make the wearer invisible in the checkered sun and shadow of the forest—the perfect camouflage of the wilderness.

Generations after Smith the Englishmen had not yet learned that lesson. For years their brilliant uniforms were targets for the red man.

Smith's eyes traveled down Powhatan's robe to the women at his feet, looking, as he was always looking, to see if they wore gems or silver or gold.

He became suddenly aware of a young girl, slim as a river reed, clad in soft buckskin, with a cape lined with the soft plumage of birds. Her blue-black hair was almost covered by a long white plume. For a second her dark eyes rested upon him, wide eyes, wistful as a fawn's.

Powhatan was listening to the red captors. Now and again he gave a signal, and there was swift obedience. A squaw brought to the weary and grimy Captain a large bowl of water and for a towel a long sheaf of feathers.

Soon there was a great feast, with speeches and with songs.

Powhatan talked with Smith, but the talk is unrecorded. Neither could understand the other very well. During these festivities Smith did manage to learn that the young maid with the white plume was Powhatan's daughter, the Princess Pocahontas.

All, to this moment, had seemed on the friendly side, but now Powhatan was holding council with his warriors—and dark glances were cast towards the Captain.

He could understand nothing they were saying, but he understood all too well when rough hands were laid upon him and he was tightly bound, his head lying on a long stone before the platform. Men appeared above him armed with heavy clubs.

Now, surely, his hour had come.

If only in this hour he could see the little princess, her dark eyes above the soft feathers; but he was too tightly bound. He could only look upward, at the smoky slanting rafters of the roof; and then at the bronzed hands holding the clubs above his head.

He clenched his teeth. At least, that lovely maid must see he died bravely and in silence. He tried to remember her face, to think of nothing else.

Suddenly, the very walls echoed with a long, piteous wail, and he could no longer see the rafters. A soft blackness of silky hair falling over his face blotted them out, a warm, wet cheek was against his own. Small hands clutched his broad shoulders.

There was a sharp, guttural order, and the upraised clubs came down heavily upon the hard-packed earth. Smith felt the very earth shake. Quick fingers were unloosing the thongs on his cramped wrists, strong hands were helping him to his feet.

Before him he saw Powhatan, his stern face half angry, half puzzled. At his feet was the Princess Pocahontas, pleading, sobbing.

Smith was led away. As the deerskin was lifted at

the entrance, he looked back. The princess was still on her knees, her great eyes following him—they were shining with tears.

More food, water, and a bed of soft skins were given him; his guards lay down and slept. So too, exhausted, did Captain Smith.

In the morning, a face ugly beyond belief bent over him as he woke. It was Powhatan, painted almost beyond recognition. Smith feared some new council, some further judgment. But he was soon reassured.

He was to be an adopted son of the tribe for all time. He was now to be guided back to Jamestown in safety by twelve of Powhatan's finest men.

The chief had one request to make. He would like a slight ransom, or gift, for the return of so brave a man as Captain Smith. The white man possessed certain things the red man would like to have.

Could he send back two of those guns like the ones on the fort. Two—and a grindstone?

Smith, when he finally understood, was quick to say yes.

He had hoped to see the princess once more. He wished he had some gift to please her, but he had only the clothes he wore, and those were more rags now than clothes. Well, Newport was overdue; per-

haps, when the ship came, he could find something among those new supplies from England.

His escort appeared at the doorway, and he bade farewell to Powhatan.

No doubt the Princess, shyly hidden, watched his stalwart figure until it was lost in the shadows of the dark woods.

She knew what he could not: She would see him again.

THE RANSOM

7

THE shallop, weeks before, had gone back to Jamestown. The men who had been left to guard it were sure Captain Smith and his two companions were dead. Smith had forbidden them to leave the shallop, but when they did so an arrow from an unseen bow had killed one of the group. Then they had heard two musket shots. After that they had waited a long time —longer than it would take even wounded men to reach the shallop again.

Without Smith things went badly at Jamestown. As the gray days grew colder, quarrels waxed hotter; food was getting low.

Then one day a sentry on the fort at Jamestown gave a sudden cry of alarm. He had seen an Indian at the edge of the forest, then another. The men of the colony seized their muskets, only to drop them in amazement at an English shout. The Captain, with his red escort, emerged into the clearing.

Most of the men rushed to meet him, overjoyed at his return. Only a few held back. Among these were Wingfield and Ratcliffe, who greeted him with coldness and ill-concealed dismay.

Now came that ticklish affair of the ransom. Smith asked that the red guests be fed, while he took a moment in which to change his tattered clothes. He wanted that moment to think out a plan, but he was soon back.

Obligingly he loaded one of the cannon not with shot, but with the largest stones possible. These he fired at an immense, ice-coated tree. The terrific noise was followed by flying stones, flying branches, flying ice, and—flying red men.

Slowly the Indians gathered together and there was much muttering among them. They were not sure, after all, that they wanted the cannon; in fact,

they were quite sure they did not. Nor, after several efforts to lift the grindstone, did they want that, either. The red men always disliked carrying heavy burdens.

Perhaps the Captain could give them things less dangerous, less weighty, to carry back to Powhatan.

Most graciously and gladly the Captain did, and they departed, well content. There is no record of the gifts, but there were no weapons among them.

As time passed, the food supply became still lower. Would Newport never arrive from England with the stores that the colony needed so badly?

At last, at last, came a shout from the water's edge. George Percy thought he saw a sail a long way off. With the pale winter sunlight upon it, it looked like a soap bubble. Men strained their eyes. Hearts rose, sank, then rose again. There was no question now! The soap bubble was dissolving itself into real shapes. It was becoming the square outlines of sails, then swaying mastheads, then the network of stout rigging. Every man in Jamestown was now on the river bank. It was, indeed, a ship. To someone with keen eyes her name became clear—the "Francis and John."

There were more men on those decks then merely

crew—many, many more, crowding the high bulwarks—new settlers to strengthen this forlorn, struggling little colony.

If the land received the newcomers coldly, certainly the Jamestown men did not. Their welcome was as warm as the circumstances permitted. Cabins were generously shared, and with Newport's new supplies there was, for the moment, enough food for everyone.

A few months later another sail was sighted—the "Phoenix." On her there were more food and more colonists.

Because the day was bitterly cold, someone anxious to make the new Englishmen more comfortable built a fire. It was probably too large a fire. A sudden wind sent the flames roaring higher and higher, spreading even on the icy, muddy ground.

Lines of men formed to the river, and buckets went swiftly back and forth. It was too late. The flames caught tree after tree, and then the fire spread to the reed-thatched roofs of cabins. Above the roar of the flames came desperate orders.

"Get the food from the storehouse!"—and men staggered through blinding smoke to obey.

"Water on the fort!"—someone shouted. "Let the cabins go!"

They prayed for rain, snow, sleet, but none came.

Cabin after cabin became a small furnace, crumpling slowly into gray ash. Most of the settlement burned completely; they had only managed to save a portion of precious food.

But the coming of those last ships with new colonists had given Jamestown new heart. Discomforts were laughed at. Cheerfully men went about the heavy task of building anew.

Captain Newport had brought with him from England new orders from the London Company. Now, instead of consulting Wingfield or Ratcliffe, he chose to talk to Smith.

Save for that one time on the ship—and there is good reason to believe Smith's imprisonment was forced on Newport—these two men seemed always to be friends. Experienced seaman and seasoned soldier, they regarded each other with respect and trust.

The London Company, said Newport, did not understand the conditions in the Virginia wilderness. All those reports of rivers had but stirred the Company to a firmer belief that one of them must be the passage that led across the land to the Western Ocean, and thence to Cathay. England must be the first to find that passage.

As for gold, the Spaniards had found quantities of it in the New World. They had also discovered silver and gems, and waters rich in pearls. Why not England?

Newport stopped and shrugged his shoulders. Then he asked, "Has that great chieftain, Powhatan, had anything to say about a possible passage through the land to a western sea?"

Smith had not asked, for there had been no time. Powhatan had spared his life and he had been glad to escape with it.

Newport thought some exploring would be good so that he could have something to report to the London Company besides that awful fire. Perhaps they could include a visit to Powhatan.

Smith agreed eagerly. Yes, he could find the way to Powhatan's camp by water if they sailed down the James into Chesapeake Bay. From there they would travel up the Pamunkey River to Werowocomoco, where dwelt Powhatan and his daughter.

They had to wait on the weather and Smith fumed with impatience. He was anxious to make a map to send back to London.

Never, Newport told the Company later, could you find a man more bent on exploring than Captain Smith. No hardship was too much for him, no danger too great.

The weather cleared at last and down the broad

James they went, rounding Point Comfort. Then they continued up the Pamunkey River until a blue haze of smoke above a bluff told them they had come to Werowocomoco.

Powhatan received them civilly. He had been anxious to see Captain Newport, who sailed those large, white-winged ships across the wide ocean. Food and shelter of the best he had to offer were given them. Nor was he unwilling to talk. What he said convinced them there was indeed a great sea to the west. It would take many days to reach it, Powhatan told them, and they would need guides and much equipment. What lay beyond that western sea he did not know.

At last Smith and Newport started back without having seen the little princess. Smith was very silent on the homeward journey, but when weather allowed, he was much engaged on a map. It was a fine map, and Captain Newport admired it greatly. Proudly he would lay it before the members of the Company and try to explain the vast distances in this New World: the swift streams with their tricky currents; the mighty, trackless forests.

8

SO BACK to Jamestown they came. Things were going well. Spring was on the way and new settlers and old were energetically rebuilding. The air rang with the cheery racket of axe and hammer. The odor of ashes was replaced by the sharp fragrance of new-cut lumber. The new cabins were better built. There was a fine new storehouse, a larger church.

With the melting of the snows, the Indians had

been coming again, in friendly mood, with quantities of food and furs for trading.

Buds were thick on the trees. Not a day passed without a new flutter of wings and bird calls. The river ran silver with fish.

When Newport prepared to sail for England, Edward-Maria Wingfield requested passage with him. Whatever Wingfield's worth, he could never be a success here for never was any man less fitted for life in the wilderness.

Wingfield's departure would leave the little-liked Ratcliffe as president; but Newport knew John Smith had been, for long, the real leader. He would not fail.

The Jamestown men gathered to watch Newport's ships go; to shout wishes for a good voyage and a swift return to the colony.

When Smith saw the sails go beyond the horizon, his eyes turned again to the forest.

There is an old, old Indian legend that in the earliest of spring days, when snow still lingers in the shady places, there comes an Indian goddess to tell all men that winter has truly gone. Swift and light she travels on the moist earth, and where her feet touch spring the frail waxen blossoms of the arbutus. Very young she is, and very fair to look upon,

with hair shining like a blackbird's wing, and the gentle eyes of a fawn.

Like her must the Princess Pocahontas have seemed to Captain Smith when, with her long train of women, she stepped shyly from the shadowy forest into the clearing at Jamestown.

The Captain leaves no record of that meeting, or of any other. She came again and again, bringing food. While the squaws laid down their burdens, and received brightly colored cloths and beads from the white man's stores, Pocahontas stood apart, her dark eyes seeking the tall Captain. Sometimes he was not there, but often she would see him drilling his men, overseeing the building, inspecting the cannon —his straight figure dark against the silver of the river water.

On one of her visits, Smith noticed that the princess was not very tall. But she was not yet a woman grown—perhaps fifteen, or less? Somewhat sadly, he reminded himself that he was nearing thirty.

The restless Captain was going on another exploring trip—he wanted to go northward up the Chesapeake. Already a boat was being made ready.

Pocahontas wondered—why, why, must it always be her tall soldier who had to risk storm and danger and possible death? There were other men, numbers of others, but she admired him the more for his brave spirit.

While she looked on with troubled eyes, John Smith and a few strong men started off in an open boat. Down the James they sailed, then into the Chesapeake and across that wide bay and around Cape Charles where the Atlantic sent its rough breakers crashing about a cluster of little islands. These they named Smith's Islands, for their leader. Then they landed on the mainland, and met friendly Indians who led them to their chief—the chief of Accomac.

Despite the discomfort of the boat, and little equipment, Smith worked on his maps, noting each jutting bit of land, each stream however small.

Then they rounded Cape Charles into the Chesapeake again and started northward. The weather grew stormy and waves came over the sides. Only incessant bailing kept the little craft afloat. More than once it was almost overturned. Their store of watersoaked bread soured and mildewed. It was impossible to eat, and with all this water around them, their drinking supply was almost gone.

The storms passed, but even Smith agreed they must make a landing where a beach and a wooded shore promised a temporary harbor. They were rowing landward when from those silent woods sprang Indian after Indian, hideously painted and howling like demons.

After a few musket shots, the red men threw down their bows as a sign of friendship. So the weary, drenched men went ashore and were given generous quantities of food as well as water.

Some of the men would have liked to return to Jamestown, but Smith had set out to go northward and northward they would go. Again they took up the heavy oars. Before them the Chesapeake lay quiet, blue and shimmering in the sun.

What a country for rivers this was! They had passed the Pamunkey, the Rappahannock; now here was another one, wide and inviting, the Potomac. Into it they turned, and went on and on, mile after mile, in silence.

Those toiling men at the oars could not know it, but where loomed before them only dense forest and small green clearings, now stands the city of Washington. Then deer grazed peacefully in the clearings, bears lumbered from the wood to seek fish; beavers worked busily at the water's edge.

One of the rowers almost dropped his oar; he was on his feet, shouting, pointing.

The sands here were no longer white—they were strangely sparkling—glittering, golden.

There was a hasty landing, and some of the sand was gathered. Then the exploring party returned downstream and back to those kindly Indians who had given them water and food.

Gold? Gold?

The red men seemed to understand. They signaled to the Englishmen to follow and padded before them up a small creek. Here, indeed, was a small mine, and the rocks shone with the same golden luster as had those sands on the shore.

Certainly the white men could have some—all they wanted. Back they toiled, heavy laden. Their boat sunk low under the burden, but high hopes gave added strength to those stout arms at the oars. Gold, gold, at last!

They rowed with a will toward Jamestown.

There were bursts of talk, then long silences as the men dreamed, perhaps, of a cottage and land of their own. No, that was not enough. With such gold a man could own a manor house, like the great ones in England; a coach and four fine horses; clothes of silk and velvet, rich with fur.

With all their dreaming, no one noticed the steady

ebbing of the tide, and near the Rappahannock the
overladen boat ran onto a sandy reef. But a survey
showed them that the high tide would easily take them
off.

All of them became aware that they were hungry,
and set to fishing.

Captain Smith gave a mighty heave, and a sudden
shout of pain. No fish had he caught, but the dread
and dangerous sting-ray; one of its barbed spines had
pierced his wrist. The wrist swelled, then the hand,
the muscular arm, and the pain grew to agony.

The men huddled miserably about him. He had
been their leader through many trials. It was he, in
those dark days, who had gone to ask the Indians for
corn.

They feared he was dying, and so did he. Still a
leader, he ordered his burial to be on a near-by island.

He lay very still, and the men held their breath.
The sun set and the brief twilight of the south descended. From the banks came the mournful crying
of the whippoorwill, the dismal quaver of the screech
owl.

They shuddered, for to red man and white alike,
that cry of the owl spoke of death.

A man leaned closer. The fearful swelling was going down; the pain must be easing, too. Gently he touched the broad chest and rose, smiling. The Captain was breathing easily. Exhausted, he had gone to sleep.

Someone lit a lantern, and the Captain woke.

Of course he was all right! He answered the eager questions almost gruffly. But he was extremely hungry. No, he did not want any regular fish. He wanted a good slice of that wretched beast which had stabbed him. When it was duly cooked, he ate it with relish.

Now the tide was coming steadily in. Soon the boat lifted from the sands and rode again in deep water.

The men rowed tirelessly. When once more they reached the familiar river and the brown palisades of Jamestown, they clambered ashore, fairly bursting with news.

Eager hands lifted the shining ore from the boat— they turned the pieces over and over; stroking them, holding them this way and that, to catch the light. Questions came like hailstones.

Gold! Gold! Gold!

They talked of nothing else.

9

———————

THIS discovery of shining ore certainly made the Jamestown men happier, but it had also its bad side. If gold had been found in one place, why not in another? They spent much time wandering in the forest up and down the river; into small creeks, hammering at rocks here, there, everywhere. They asked questions of every Indian they met, of all those who came into Jamestown.

Smith was uneasy. He wanted more clearings made

77

for planting and more cabins built, for Newport was expected soon with more colonists.

It was only September, but soon the frosts would come and, all too swiftly, the winter.

The Indians were still bringing food, but with the cold weather their visits would stop.

If the settlers did not cease their everlasting rock pounding, it was likely that the Indians would not come at all. The noise scared the game, and that always annoyed the red men.

Smith had but one pleasure these days; now and again Pocahontas came, when her tribe brought food. Her visits were ever a joy to the worried Captain.

He asked about Powhatan's health. Yes, her father was well—she seemed about to say more, but did not. It made Smith more uneasy; he wished Newport would come.

Soon the exultant cry of a sail sighted rang through the settlement and, as always, every man sped to the water's edge.

There was ever excitement when a ship came, but the "Mary and Margaret," easing in to the shore, caused more than usual.

A murmur ran through the crowd—could they be seeing aright? Among the people on the decks there seemed to be the flutter of wide skirts. The sun shone on snowy, ruffled caps.

A sailor who leaped ashore with a heavy rope was surrounded by questioners.

"Yes," he replied, "Mistress Thomas Forest has come out with her husband. The other one is her maid, Anne Burras."

Suddenly the men wished they were cleaner, better shaven. Hastily they brushed at their worn clothing and stamped mud from their boots.

To Mistress Forest and young Anne Burras that landing must have been a little embarrassing. There were so many eager hands held out to help them, so many staring eyes, but the Jamestown men, try as they might, could not help staring. It had been a long time since they had seen the fair faces of English women. This, indeed, was a wonderful sight.

Each man wished his cabin were neater, and tried to remember how he had left it.

For a moment, the sight of the feminine faces overshadowed all else; but now Newport was ashore, and Smith hurried to greet him.

Soon introductions were being made, for there was a goodly company on this ship. There were men well known in old England—in politics, at court;

soldiers seasoned in many wars. That they were casting their lot with the Virginia colony was a good sign.

A little apart stood a group of eight men who acknowledged greetings solemnly, and in a strange tongue. Poles and Germans they were; the first foreigners in English Virginia, and they knew how to make pitch and tar and glass.

Smith eyed them with favor; such skilled workers were needed indeed.

Now, besides the familiar rolls of cloth, the cases and bags of food, the heavy boxes of firearms and ammunition, most unfamiliar packages were coming up from the hold.

Newport, with a half smile, spoke quietly to Smith: "Presents for Powhatan."

He would explain later, but now there must be temporary housing and food for the newcomers.

Mercifully the weather was balmy. The forest, gay with the crimson and gold of its autumn leafage, looked less dark and somber.

Around glowing fires some of the men talked long about the gold which had been found. While they talked, the old settlers hoped the Indians would come soon. Of course all Englishmen knew venison, but the taste of wild turkey could not be described. It was a real treat. And the sweet Indian corn from which they made their bread was far, far better than wheat.

It was late before Smith and Newport could get together; even later before they parted. There was much to discuss.

The new orders from the London Company were still most insistent about gold; Newport did hope this new-found ore contained it.

As usual, there was a demand for the route to the Western Ocean and, something new—to search for that long-lost colony at Roanoke. All of these demands meant more exploring, and both men liked that.

And—those gifts must be taken to Powhatan.

Again and again had Newport tried to explain the American red man to the English at home, but in vain. If this mighty chieftain, Powhatan, was ruler of all Virginia, then a king he must be, and would like gifts befitting a monarch.

So a very handsome bedstead had been sent. The gift of a bedstead was less fantastic in the seventeenth century than it sounds to modern ears. Bedsteads were possessed only by the wealthy; the majority of folk slept on pallets on the floor; the poorer on rags and rushes.

Smith nodded. Powhatan would probably prefer

his own bed of fragrant pine boughs, covered by smooth deerskins, and furs for covering.

However, he would, no doubt, use the bedstead for a throne. Smith remembered with a shudder lying bound before that crude, so-called throne of Powhatan's. He remembered too the soft hair falling over his face, the warm wet cheek, the clutching small hands. He tried to forget, while Newport went on to tell about the other gifts he had brought.

There were a most beautiful pitcher and basin, an elaborately gilded crown, and a robe richly embroidered with flowers and leaves and gold thread.

The two friends probably laughed a little, remembering the grim face of the chieftain, the stiff crest of hair with its proud eagle feathers, symbol of a warrior; the simple robes of buckskin and furs.

But the chief would doubtless be pleased.

Newport asked if Powhatan was still friendly. Smith hesitated, then replied that he seemed to be, for food still came. But Smith had learned, long since, that the Indian temper was uncertain. He had also noticed that friendliness grew when the colony was small. Too many white men seemed to alarm the red men. Of course if there were ever enough really to withstand an Indian attack, all would be well. Newport had heard the Company expected to send many, many more.

Now they must sleep. In the morning, they would prepare for explorations, before the cold came.

The newcomers were busily building when Smith and Newport left, and perhaps no man ever had so much assistance offered as did Master Thomas Forest, the man who had brought a wife to the colony. Anything to be near those English women, to gaze at the crisply ruffled caps, the rustling skirts; to receive praise and thanks from the grateful women for their labors.

If all the men were gallant, one John Laydon, listed on the ship lists as a laborer, was more so. Even after the women were well housed, he was ever about to help young Anne with water buckets and with the firewood. At last, Anne came to Mistress Forest with news that her mistress had already guessed.

She and John would like to marry.

The news spread—a wedding, the first wedding in Virginia!

Willing hands helped to build a new cabin; to decorate the church. Not a flower was to be found

in those dark days, but there were evergreen boughs
and berries a-plenty. The whole company of Jamestown crowded into the crude log church.

Smith and Newport returned as the first snows fell.
No new gold, no quick passage to the western sea, no
news of Roanoke.

It was now time for Newport to return to England.
Before he sailed a council was held, and Smith for-
mally elected president.

He and Newport looked over the stores with care.
There was none too much, with the winter before
them. Smith had another reason for being unhappy.
Some of the new colonists were excellent men. The
others? Well, neither he nor Newport could understand the policy of the Company. If men had not
been too good in England, why should they, under
harder conditions, be of value in the New World?

Newport sailed away in the dreary month of December. He would once again try to explain the conditions in this new world. But for good measure he
took with him a carefully written letter from the new
president.

Respectfully, but firmly, Smith requested that the
Company send "carpenters, husbandmen gardeners,
fishermen, blacksmiths, masons," and, he ended
somewhat desperately, "diggers up of trees' roots."

10

TOWARD Christmas, of all times, the food was getting dangerously low. There was nothing to do but go to the Indians and try to get corn before the worst weather came.

A small boat was loaded with a scant store of food and some stores for trading. In it Smith, George Percy, young Francis West and a few picked men set forth, but they had waited a trifle too late. By the time they had reached Hampton, where dwelt a small Indian tribe called the Kecoughtans, they were obliged to stop. Blinding snow and stinging sleet were falling. The men were soon drenched to the skin, shaking with cold, and desperately hungry.

Here at Hampton they were forced to spend Christmas. Fortunately the Kecoughtans were friendly, and, as one of the Englishmen wrote later, never, even in old England, had they had finer Christmas fare. There were oysters and fish, wild turkey and venison, and bread made of the sweet corn meal.

No doubt the white men tried to explain the festival of Christmas to the red hosts. How well they succeeded no one knows. The idea of a feast was understandable, for the red man had many of his own. There were feasts for the spring planting, the autumn harvest, the first fishing, and the first hunting. But the Indian could not understand the white man's religion.

It is possible they might have liked that story of the great, shining star, but language was limited, and there was no star to point to this Christmas-tide —only the swirling snow.

Friendly as the Kecoughtans were, they were a very small tribe and had no extra stores for trade. Indeed, they had barely enough for their own winter needs. So, when the weather broke, the Englishmen went up the Pamunkey towards the village of Powhatan. They camped in an empty hut near by, and asked some Indians to take a message to the chief, Powhatan.

When the messengers returned, Powhatan's reply was vague. He had no spare corn, but he might be able to get some from another tribe. As for food, why did not the white brothers come to his village and eat there?

Smith had never trusted Powhatan and there was something about this message he did not like. As usual, his instincts were right.

That night every man was wakened by a slight sound outside the hut. Smith was first on his feet, first at the entrance.

In the dimness he saw bundles by the entrance— a great haunch of venison and a basket of corn. Then he heard a low voice, like bubbling brook water, whispering, pleading.

"Do not come! My father means ill—his mood is again unfriendly. This was all the food I could gather without my father's knowledge." Pocahontas's soft voice broke a little. "Captain, go back to Jamestown."

And then she was gone, back into the forest shadows.

All that night, all the next nights, all his life, Smith would hear that little, low voice.

He bade his men sleep. They would talk in the morning. He himself did not sleep. They could not return to Jamestown without food. They must go to Powhatan, come what may. But he was more than grateful for that whispered warning.

At dawn Smith consulted with his men. They agreed that they must go.

"Let the men keep close together," Smith warned. "Have your muskets ready. Let no red men get behind you."

They had a chance, he added. The Indians were quick to change, and even Powhatan had a wholesome fear of English firearms.

So, watchfully, they went to the Indian village. The old chieftain was not openly unfriendly. "Will not the white brothers lay aside those heavy firearms?" he asked. "We shall eat and then discuss this matter of corn."

The Englishmen laid their firearms aside—but conveniently near.

They ate as only strong men can eat in the face of danger.

Then, ever alert, they followed Powhatan and his

warriors into that long house where the chief held court.

History does not record if the carved English bedstead had replaced the former rough-hewn throne; most likely it had.

Now Powhatan spoke about the corn. He himself had not enough to spare any to the Englishmen, but he knew of a tribe that had had a rich harvest. He had consulted with them by messenger.

He could get forty large baskets of corn for the English, but only for a certain price. Although this other tribe wanted neither cloth nor beads nor hatchets, they insisted on one fine English sword for each basket.

Smith turned to his men. They drew closer and picked up their muskets as if to leave. Smith fingered the heavy pistol in his belt, as if thinking. He came closer, drew the heavy weapon from its case. He hated to make this threatening move, for the man before him was, after all, the father of the little princess. But the thought of those sharp swords in merciless red hands, the thought of the waiting men at Jamestown, forced him to go on.

The red chieftain looked at the pistol held so close to him. Then he gazed squarely at this fearless Englishman. He feared him, hated him, admired him. And full well he knew that the tale of that other tribe had not deceived him.

Captain Smith returned the stare. He spoke with decision.

"No swords," he said. "We shall try elsewhere for corn."

Powhatan thought. That would be most difficult for the English brothers. Perhaps, after all, he could secure some corn, if they would stay a few days?

They stayed—ever on the alert—their muskets ever ready.

The corn was remarkably quick in coming, considering the tale of the unknown tribe at some distance away, but no questions were asked. The boat was speedily loaded. Around the goods for trade clustered eager red men, bargaining for lengths of bright cloth, strings of colored beads, hatchets, shining nails. And down the Pamunkey River went the Englishmen.

Now, with great care, the settlers would not starve this winter. The cold had come early; sometimes, in this new land, that meant an early spring.

Captain Smith and his men were met at Jamestown with relief. Willing hands unloaded the corn, and eager ears listened to the account of the strange Christmas at Kecoughtan.

Smith carefully looked over the stores of ammunition, ordered more sentries, and gave stern orders. The river and the forest must both be watched all day, all night. The men obeyed without question this Captain who had again risked his life to bring them food.

There were some good days in February and in March there were fish in the river. On all the good days the settlers worked with a will. They made weirs along the river bank for catching fish. They repaired old cabins and built some new ones. They dug a well which, after much toil, gave good water, sweet and fresh; and as soon as the frosts melted from the hard earth, they started clearing more acres for the spring planting.

What a heartening time was spring! Every evening, when they gathered for a small meal, each man had something to tell. One had seen a few ducks on the river. A sentry on night duty thought he had heard geese passing overhead. A man clearing trees came in at sunset with a tiny bunch of violets in his calloused hand.

Where the first pale leafbuds were coming out on the trees, there came that most welcome of shouts: "A sail, a sail!"

Smith's heart leaped—Newport!

It was not Newport, but a total stranger. Captain Samuel Argall was a swaggering young man, with hard eyes. He had a few stores but no colonists in his small ship.

However, he had much information to give out.

As everyone knew, he told them, all the vessels to this new land of Virginia had gone southward to the West Indies, then northward again. It was a long and tedious voyage, and very expensive. But there were other ways to cross the ocean. His listeners would remember that some years ago, Captain Bartholomew Gosnold had sailed across the Atlantic to the place, far north, which he had named Cape Cod? They would remember, too, that the fishing fleets of all nations went across each year to the Grand Banks?

He, Captain Argall, had, for the London Company, tried the direct route taken by the fishing fleets. The trip had taken only nine weeks; and, but for two weeks in which there was not enough wind to fill a sail, he could have made it in seven.

Jamestown buzzed with talk. This new route would bring their supplies so much, much, quicker. Better still, they would not feel so far away from England.

When the excitement died down, Argall was besieged with questions. The most important was about that gold. Argall shrugged. It was not only not gold, but no metal of any value at all!

This was depressing, but not for long. All talk was of that new, shorter sea route.

Captain Smith asked one question only. He wanted news of Captain Newport and what he heard was cheering.

Captain Newport was to come out with some of the new colonists. Even now the ship he was to command was almost ready in the shipyards. It was a brave ship with a brave name, the "Sea Venture."

11

IT WAS June when the colonists left England to try Captain Argall's new route, and hopes were high indeed over its shortness. There were seven ships and about five hundred colonists and, contrary to the usual custom, not only men but also a fair number of women and children.

On Christopher Newport's vessel was the Admiral of the fleet, Somers, and Governor Gates, who was being sent to relieve Captain Smith.

Straight across the Atlantic, with but a pause at the Canary Islands, came the little fleet for seven weeks. Two more weeks should bring them into the great Bay, into the wide river, and to Jamestown.

Then on Saint James' Day the skies grew suddenly black. There was terrifying lightning and thunder. So swiftly did the winds come that not even the brawny arms of a dozen men could hold the great tillers. Gales tossed the ships about like toys. Sails were torn into flapping ribbons before they could be lowered. Stout masts cracked like kindling wood, and heavy crosstrees came flying down like splinters.

With horror, the travelers saw one ship reel and go down. Blinding rains blotted out the others. They could only see their own vessels; no more.

With the clearing, five beaten and disabled ships tossed upon the water. There was no sign of the "Sea Venture" which had been carrying their leaders, Newport, Somers, and Gates. No one had seen her sink. She simply wasn't there.

The men on the remaining five vessels patched the sails and masts as best they could, for there was a chance that they might yet reach Virginia.

In the gray daybreak after that storm the men of

the "Sea Venture" strained their eyes in vain for
the sight of another sail. Captain Newport consulted
what charts he had. He thought they were some-
where off that Spanish land called Florida, for he
knew his ship had been blown far southward. The
wind blew strongly, steadily, from the north. Many
times they could only drift, but Newport ordered
masts repaired and sails patched. Again he consulted that small store of charts.

Then he had a sudden idea. Possibly they were
near that island in midocean, he suggested to Admiral Somers—that island so aptly described as
"thousands of miles from anywhere," Bermuda. At
least, that lonely island was not inhabited. It belonged to no one. Even if the winds permitted they
could not land on Spanish Florida, and they certainly did not wish to be driven still farther south to the
Spanish West Indies. Spain was already angry
enough about Virginia. She would show little mercy
to an English ship.

Suddenly Newport became aware of a sailor waiting respectfully behind him. Those quick seaman's
ears had caught the word Bermuda. He did not keep
it to himself. It spread through the ship with the
speed of fire.

The crew were uneasy, fearful. Their talk had

managed to alarm many of the passengers. But it was a few chosen men of the crew who came protesting to Captain Newport. The Captain must know that this island of Bermuda bore a bad reputation. As the Isle of Devils it had, for years, been avoided by all seamen. Here dwelt demons who snarled and roared in dense forests, who raced shrieking and wailing along the shores, awaiting unwary sailors.

Newport's orders grew sharper. Would they prefer to die of hunger and thirst in a leaking ship? He had never seen this island of Bermuda, but he had not been in the West Indies for nothing. He did know that once upon a time savage Indians had dwelt there, but they had been captured by a Spanish captain and sent, as slaves, to work in the mines of Mexico and of Peru. At least, there would be no Indian foes to contend with.

As for the demons, Captain Newport held no faith in demons. Would the leadsman make constant soundings of the depth of the water, the lookouts watch for rock and reef? Land was land.

"Shoal sho—al wa—ter!" called the leadsman suddenly.

"Rocks! Reefs! Rocks!" came the shout from a lookout on a patched mast.

Both warnings came too late; the "Sea Venture" struck, shuddered, and men fell sprawling on the slanting deck. They had struck a reef. In fact, they were wedged between two. Jagged points tore into the ship's sides, and water poured in. There was an order to the pumps, but it was too late. The order was quickly changed—"lower the boats"!

The people aboard could hear timbers cracking. They could see the drenched decks settling lower and lower. There were anxious questions. Was it the Isle of Devils? Newport's reply was brief, and the same as before. Land was land!

No life was lost in that perilous landing for the "Sea Venture" had a picked crew. Her colonists were of the best; so too were the three leaders, Newport, Somers, and Gates.

The shipwrecked travelers soon found themselves on an island so beautiful it might well have been enchanted, but hardly by demons. Now that they could face water without fear, they saw these seas to be blue as sapphires. The men were quick to realize that the millions of sea birds were the so-called screaming devils of the shore. The snarling demons of the forests were only herds of wild pigs, descendants of swine left long ago by some Spanish ship.

The air was soft and balmy; there was game in plenty, fish in shoals.

Soon every man was at work, cautiously going out in the longboats to salvage what they could from the wrecked ship—clothing and food, tools and timbers and metal. The ship's bell was brought, and called all to a prayer that was led by the chaplain, Master Buck. On the white sands of that lonely island they knelt to give grateful thanks for this deliverance from the fury of the sea. Hymns mingled with the cries of the wheeling sea birds.

One passenger on that ship is nameless, but he has come down in history as a valuable member of the little colony on Bermuda—a dog. It may be judged he was a large animal, and a brave one, for he straightaway set about his self-appointed duties in the woods, bringing down one wild pig after another.

So the Bermuda folk had, in addition to fish and fowl, an almost forgotten delicacy—the juicy sweetness of fresh pork.

After the long labors of the day, they gathered about the campfires. Captain Newport warned them to look out for a possible Spanish ship. It was not the Spaniards' usual route from the Indies, but one could never tell.

Steadily the men worked to build shelters. They

waited for heat to come, but it did not; nor did those fevers which had killed so many at Jamestown. Later they expected cold, but there was never much change in the weather.

They could, had they so chosen, have lived out their lives on this lovely island, but they had set out for Virginia and to Virginia they wished to go.

Vigorously they set about the building of two strong pinnaces, made from the excellent lumber on the island and certain needful things saved from the "Sea Venture." It was slow, hard work, and ten months passed before the little vessels were ready to sail northward toward Virginia.

Weather and wind favored them, but it was a long voyage, and Newport was plied with further questions.

He was cautious in his answers. They must not expect too much of Jamestown; it was still but a crude settlement, nor was the climate so gentle as that of Bermuda. There was heat, sultry and stifling, and bleak and biting cold. The more adventurous people were especially curious about the Indians. Somewhat sourly Newport replied that in all likehood they would see more than enough of those red men.

Nevertheless, he felt a certain pride in Virginia. After all, he had brought out some of the first colonists. He remembered the blossoming glory of the land that spring of 1607—the beauty of dogwood and redbud, the flower-starred meadows, the pungent sweetness of wild strawberries.

It would be later in the year before they reached land this time, but he hoped to get his passengers there before the full heat of summer.

All these months he had wondered about the other ships. Had they reached Jamestown, or had they gone down in deep waters? Perhaps, like themselves, the others had been marooned on some lonely coast. Admiral Somers and Governor Gates shared these fears, but they said nothing to the others.

Now the Bermuda colonists talked eagerly of reaching a real English colony, of greeting old friends once more.

From the Atlantic they turned into Chesapeake Bay, then into the James River. There was admiration of that wide river and the great forests. Now and again, in some meadow, they saw wild deer, lumbering bears and beavers busy on their dams at the edge of the water.

Newport told how the Jamestown men watched

for a sail; how they gathered at the bank with shouts of welcome. Seasoned mariner that he was, his heart beat a little faster as they passed landmarks he knew so well.

What a tale he would have to tell his good friend, John Smith!

12

TWO years ago this Maytime had John Smith, a prisoner, first seen the land of Virgina. Now he was president of the council and leader of the colony. He looked about with some satisfaction at the sturdy fort with its cannon, at the rows of cabins, at the acres of newly planted rich earth. Of late the

107

Indians had been quiet. Sometimes they came in to trade. Now and again came the little princess.

On that last visit to Powhatan the old Chieftain had asked Smith a direct, a disturbing question.

When were the Englishmen leaving?

Smith's reply is not recorded, but it was probably equally direct. "The Englishmen have come to stay."

That question kept coming back into Smith's mind, as annoying and persistent as the whine and sting of a mosquito.

Now there was a new anxiety. Where was Captain Newport and that promised fleet of ships and settlers and supplies? Argall had said they were almost ready when he had left England. Since then, Argall had gone back. It seemed a good season for a swift crossing on the new route. Perhaps too calm. Many weeks had gone by.

Work went on peacefully at Jamestown. Most of the last colonists sent out were good men. The idlers and malcontents were a mere handful, and they received little sympathy or support.

The newcomers were getting used to the summer heat. The corn was a waving sea of green.

Then, as the weeks lengthened into months, more and more men walked the river's edge, watching for a sail.

It was August before the longed-for shouts arose.

One—two—three—another—four—and yet another—five!

How very slowly they were coming up the river! Soon the men on shore saw the reason. Some of the masts were mended, some still broken, and there were only a few patched and ragged sails.

Painfully the battered vessels creaked into shore. Aboard were haggard men and women, wailing children. How many? How many? Smith and George Percy were aghast. The fleet carried three hundred passengers, and among them were three of Smith's arch enemies of the former council, Archer, Martin, and Ratcliffe.

The unloading of passengers and stores took the first hours; then came the questions.

The new arrivals had seen one ship sunk, but the "Sea Venture" had disappeared. That was all they knew. They had seen no signs of wreckage.

The stores of all five ships held but little food. Why?

Ratcliffe replied that they had been tossing about for weeks. They had to eat. Moreover, he added with his usual insolence, a new governor, Gates, had been sent out on the "Sea Venture" to supplant Smith. Therefore Smith was no longer governor.

Despite the troubles at sea, Ratcliffe had evidently sown seeds of discontent on the way over. The Jamestown men stood solidly behind Smith; most of the newcomers behind Ratcliffe.

Smith was desperate. At once he sent some of Ratcliffe's men to Nansemond, others to the Falls of the Farre West. If they disliked Smith's rule at Jamestown, they could make settlements of their own and select their own leaders.

This would be the most peaceful arrangement until Somers, Governor Gates, and Newport arrived. Smith's heart was heavy at the thought of bluff, honest Christopher Newport. He might never come at all!

At Werowocomoco Powhatan listened to guttural reports.

Five ships had come to Jamestown. Aboard were hundreds of Englishmen and, even more alarming, white squaws and white papooses. Now the red men knew that these Engishmen had come to stay, to clear more fields, to frighten the game from the forests, and thus drive the Indians ever farther westward.

Already there were too many white men to pick off one by one by Indian arrows—too many for small tribes to attack openly. Arrows were no match for

those deadly bullets, those fire-breathing cannon.

"Have the English had a good harvest?" Powhatan asked. "Excellent," was the reply, "but far from enough for all these new-come folk."

Powhatan grunted. Good. There was one way out.

He sent a message to his brother, Opechancanough, over at Paspihae and to all near-by tribes.

No food was to be given to the English; not so much as one grain of corn. It wasn't to be traded for hatchets or beads or cloth; not even for swords and muskets and cannon.

The white men must starve.

The heat of a sultry September did nothing to cool tempers. A dwindling food supply did less. A few of the new men set to work building cabins and harvesting corn; more did not. The men who worked grew rebellious. Why should they work when others did not?

Smith visited the settlements at Nansemond and the Falls; little had been done. He reminded them that despite September heat the frosts of October were soon to come, the pelting rains of November, the snows of the winter. Surely Martin, Archer and Ratcliffe must remember?

There were arguments that grew more and more

bitter. There were wore complaints than the now falling leaves of the trees or the sands of the beaches.
No one had time or patience to listen to all of them.

Some fish had been salted and dried. With the remaining corn, it lay in the storehouse. All the food in
the colony was much too small an amount for so many.

These scanty stores were well guarded, for few
men trusted each other.

The season for venison and turkey arrived, but no
laden canoes appeared upon the river. The forest
lay silent—ominous.

Smith hoped against hope that the "Sea Venture" might yet appear. Gladly indeed would he give
over his responsibilities to that new Governor, Gates,
if—if he were a good governor. Smith was weary,
but he could not give over this little colony to that
rascal, Ratcliffe. He had come to love Jamestown
too well; to feel a pride in its well-being. He could
not abandon the faithful men who had so staunchly
stood by him.

Smith called George Percy and Francis West and
some of the others—sober, thoughtful men—and they
talked long together.

There were some five hundred mouths to feed, and
winter was almost upon them, and the three men

knew how little lay in the storehouse. All agreed that the sooner the ships were repaired and sent back to England, the sooner relief might come.

But what was to be done in the meantime?

Someone suggested going to the Indians again.

George Percy announced, gravely, that they had extremely little to offer in the way of trading goods. He looked at Smith, and Smith looked grim indeed. Well he knew that so many English had already alarmed the Indians.

Had they not noticed that, all these days of autumn, when harvests were ready and hunting good, no red men had come? Had they been unaware of that strange silence?

A chorus of voices rose. Captain Smith got on so well with the Indians—surely they would trust him till the next ships came?

Smith had never felt more hopeless or more helpless, but to cheer them, he nodded. He could only try.

Suddenly he heard shouts. His name was being called as usual. A small boat was at the landing with news that the Nansemond folk were not faring well. There was some trouble at the Falls colony.

These senseless brawls had best be settled before they could manage to anger the red neighbors. Smith left at once.

13

NO EXACT records remain of Smith's interviews with the people at Nansemond and the Falls colony, but there is reason to believe that they were stormy. Tired, disgusted, discouraged, Smith started back to Jamestown.

Then, truly, that little colony experienced one of its greatest calamities. Smith's powder pouch exploded, and he was desperately wounded. He was hovering between life and death when the sailors carried him ashore. And there was no man there skilled at healing such a wound as this.

The ships, now repaired, were ready to sail for England. The only hope for Smith's recovery, and it was a scant one, was to go home. His friends insisted, and the wounded man was too weak, too wretched, to protest.

George Percy was left as president.

Powhatan listened with intense interest to spies fresh from the neighborhood of Jamestown.

The Englishmen were quarreling much among themselves. The five ships had sailed; food was being handed out carefully, and in very small quantities.

Most important of all, the great chief of the white men, the tall Captain, had been sore wounded and had gone away in one of the white winged ships.

If Powhatan ever smiled, he smiled then.

Well indeed he knew the worth, the power of the tall Captain.

A small form stirred, stiffened at Powhatan's feet, and slipped quietly away.

The little princess did not sleep that long night. She saw the moon rise and set, the stars fade before the pale dawn, the sunrise of a new day.

There were doubtless times when she sobbed in utter despair, others in which she prayed to her own gods, to the strange god of the English, to any ear which might listen——

"Let him live—let him come back!"

Winter came early that year, with bleak winds and icy rains. There was not enough shelter, so there was overcrowding; not enough warm clothing or covering or, worst of all, food. Everything made the colonists a prey to sickness. And sickness came.

Although George Percy was an experienced man, able and honest, he had a giant's task on his hands. With all his heart, he wished John Smith were here.

The quarrels increased, the work lessened, and hunger bred selfishness. A few of the braver, stronger men went hunting, but this noisy settlement had already driven the game farther into the forests.

One party brought back a solitary deer; they would share it only with their closest friends. No morsel was given to anyone else. And they had lost two men. But a few more ventured forth, and came back with two turkeys.

They had found the missing men—dead men— pierced with Indian arrows. This second party lost

three men. They had seen no Indians, but they must be all about—an arrow here, there, then a half dozen, a dozen, from unseen bows.

George Percy pondered. Was one deer worth the lives of two men; two turkeys worth the lives of three?

The days grew shorter and now the snows had come. The hunting stopped. Sickness increased with cold and hunger.

No day passed without one death, sometimes more. The stronger men wearily shoveled away the snows and hard earth for one shallow grave after another.

Percy, now ill himself, went from cabin to cabin. Some glared at him with resentful, angry eyes; others with hopeless pleading.

Then one day he could go no further; he staggered and fell. Under tattered blankets his friends strove in vain to warm him. They tried to build a fire with water-soaked wood. Then, as suddenly as he had been cold, he was hot—burning with fever.

Even though he was ill, his duties lay heavy on his mind. Bravely he strove to keep his wits about him, to give what orders he could; to keep in touch with what went on. As soon as a man entered his cabin he would open bright, feverish eyes and ask questions. It was often hard for his friends to answer those questions. They would beg him to rest, to get well.

But he could not, and would not.

Only this morning, he would insist, he had heard men passing his cabin with loads of some sort. Had the hunters gotten game again?

He insisted on answers.

No—no game—more were dead—they were burying them.

How many now?

Some two hundred—or more.

Once he had thought he heard men calling, loud and long. Had a ship come? "No!" was the answer. "Wolves have drawn close to the settlement, for even the animals can find no food."

Now and again Percy heard the wailing cry of a woman, the husky voices of brawling men. But there was more and more quiet—a strange, a dreadful quiet.

Then a change came. There was the smell of wet earth beneath rapidly melting snow. Francis West entered, a dark figure against a brilliant moon.

"Spring?" said West in answer to Percy's question. "Yes—almost—the wind has turned to the south. There is a real warmth in the sunshine."

He also announced that Ratcliffe had, with a few

men, left that day to seek corn of the red men. There was not a grain left.

More men drifted in, men terribly thin, with hollow eyes sunk deep in the sockets. They tried to avoid many subjects; of how they had chewed bark from the trees, and tough roots; of how they had eaten the only things their feeble hands could catch—lizards and snakes yet sluggish from the winter's sleep.

But Percy was better now. He noticed the wretched rags of clothing that hung from gaunt shoulder bones, the bony, shaking hands which so faithfully tried to serve him.

"How many dead, how many?" Percy asked.

It was useless to tell even a merciful lie. Percy would soon be up to see for himself.

"Some four hundred, sir," was the reply. "There are only about sixty living."

A halloo came from the river. Ratcliffe must be back with the hoped-for corn.

But Ratcliffe was not back. He lay dead on the shore of the Pamunkey River—he and several of the men. Yes—Indian arrows. . . .

The survivors clambered wearily on shore with empty hands. They received no corn.

14

SLOWLY up the James River sailed the pinnaces from Bermuda. They were strong, well-built little vessels, and the weather had favored them most of the way. But they were crowded. Fortunately the long months on that lonely island had created friendships.

Newport, remembering earlier voyages when he was perpetually called upon to settle disputes and listen to grievances, was grateful. These Bermuda folk were a good lot. They would be a welcome addition to the colony at Jamestown. Admiral Somers was dignified and competent; Governor Gates, wise, quiet, friendly.

Newport's passengers admired the towering forests, the rich meadow lands reaching to the water's edge. Some of them, back in England, had heard George Percy's reports on this lovely land. They knew they would like it. Eagerly they looked forward to Jamestown, longing to stretch weary, cramped sea legs; to feel the solid ground beneath their feet; to come to a real English town.

Once more, Captain Newport warned them not to expect too much. It was not yet an English town such as they thought of. There would be no sturdy cottages, no neat farms outlying the town; only crude huts, a church of rough-hewn logs; a few clearings to be planted with corn.

They were almost there; and Newport's eyes, the keen, far-seeing eyes of the seaman, had noted two things. Often, when he had come, he had met little boats far down the river fishing; had been hailed with joyful shouts by some hunters along the banks.

This time he had seen no one. He felt a strange, an uneasy foreboding. Now they were nearer, and the keen eyes strained for the thin threads of chimney smoke or campfires; there were none. That river, that land, seemed as deserted as the first time they had come from England two long years ago.

He said nothing—his thoughts were racing. Had that last little fleet been sunk with all its colonists, its precious stores? Or had it been marooned, as had the "Sea Venture," on some remote shore? Had the Indians come, murderous and merciless? Had the fevers of last summer been worse, or the winter's cold more impossible to bear?

Now they were coming in to the landing. Something was wrong—frightfully wrong. Two pinnaces, their hulls crusted with slimy weeds, rocked by the bank. The ropes which anchored them were rotting, frayed almost to the breaking point.

And there were no men—no shouts of welcome.

Newport turned to Gates and Somers, finding his fears reflected in their somber eyes. The passengers were happily gathering their few belongings together.

The fort was so rotted that the cannon sagged in their supports. Most of the cabins were in ruins. The clearings, which should now be green with corn, were already overgrown. The forest was creeping back.

Newport cleared a tightening throat and shouted again and again. The Bermuda folk now stood in the boats—gazing, bewildered, aghast.

And now they came forth—the men of Jamestown.

Out of the wreckage of cabins they tottered, staggered, crawled—skeletons in rags.

Only a few could speak at all—the rest only held out pitiful, bony claws. Food!

The little pinnaces had scant food left. What they had they quickly gave.

One of the skeletons came, on uncertain feet, to Captain Newport. It took him minutes to recognize George Percy.

"Smith?" asked Newport.

Percy made a brave effort to answer. "Wounded —last fall—please God, now safe in England." If only, if only, he had been here! He, Percy, had been ill—he had failed.

"No," said Newport, gently. He was sure Percy had done all which could be done. The dark, sunken eyes rested upon him gratefully.

The Bermuda men, though tired from the long voyage, were still strong. They set to with a will and soon caught some fish from the river. Then, cleaning a few rusty muskets, they brought down some small game.

That night they rested; next day they held solemn consultation.

No one had much to say; respectfully they listened

to one another. Gravely, quietly, they considered every angle of the fearful situation.

It would be a long time before the Jamestown men would have much strength to work. There were not enough of the Bermuda men to face, alone, the task of rebuilding. And there were far too few to resist an Indian attack.

Newport recalled his last visit, with Smith, to Powhatan. There had certainly been no friendliness then.

"And none since," added Percy. "They are waiting for us to starve."

It was an evil blow to the refugees from Bermuda, so long on that distant island, so long on the water.

What was to be done next? There were the two pinnaces left by the last ships. Then there were their own two that had been built in Bermuda. These could be overhauled. But could the colonists cross the wide ocean in such small vessels?

Newport had a better idea. They could hug the coast northward. At this season the fishing fleets would be off the Grand Banks. There they could get food, and possibly a passage home to England.

One and all agreed—it was the only thing to do.

Soon the four little pinnaces were ready and loaded. They made a rather forlorn little fleet, but they were leaving behind an even more forlorn sight—the wreckage of Jamestown, England's only hope in the new world.

Down the broad river, and before them lay the Chesapeake, the sunlight sparkling on its blue waters. Suddenly one of Newport's sailors gave a shout, then another. Now they could all see! Coming toward them was a longboat from some ship!

Its sailors rowed swiftly on, with long, powerful strokes. And now there was a flutter of red, of white, of blue deeper than the blue of the Bay. The English flag!

Newport turned to speak to Admiral Somers, standing beside him, but the Admiral's eyes were misted. His lips moved silently.

Some of the Jamestown men struggled to their feet; some sobbed weakly.

Now the heavy longboat was beside them, with its crew of stalwart, ruddy British sailors. For a few moments no one could understand anything—shouts, questions, answers. The sailors looked with horror and pity at the Jamestown men. Quickly they tossed bags of bread into the pinnaces.

"The 'Sea Venture'? All the way from Bermuda— the Isle of Devils?" Practiced eyes ran over the little pinnaces with admiration.

"Isle of Devils, no—no," yelled one of the Bermuda men. "It's Paradise!"

Now the talk cleared. The leader of the longboat announced that off Point Comfort lay three fine ships commanded by Lord de la Warre. New colonists were aboard with generous stores.

Silence fell—a thoughtful silence.

Then a feeble voice spoke—would Lord de la Warre take them home to England? Another voice broke in. Perhaps with new men, new stores, they could try again? More voices joined in. No! Yes! No! Yes! They had suffered too much—it could all happen again.

Newport turned to Somers, then to Gates. Newport thought the men must decide for themselves. The others agreed.

Newport hailed the other pinnaces. His men were talking things over; would all of them do the same, he asked?

The longboat rocked alongside, the sailors waiting patiently.

The talk went on—now low, now aloud; for and against.

Somers spoke at last. Some decision must be made, some report sent to Lord de la Warre. Perhaps the men so weakened from the winter at Jamestown had best go back to England when the first ships sailed? Perhaps many of the Bermuda men were weary of isolation? Make your own choice. Will you hold up your hands? How many want to go back to Jamestown?

Some hands went up at once, some with hesitation. The sunburned hands were those of the men from Bermuda. But among them was raised one bony hand, and another, and yet another. They belonged to the Jamestown men. More hands were up now, only a very few down. A voice spoke: "Back to Jamestown."

Newport started to count, counted carefully again. Only one hand remained down. A voice spoke feebly.

"I cannot raise my arm, sir—but—I want to go back."

Quickly the man next to him held up the shaking arm.

Newport turned hastily to hail the other little vessels. Across the water came the reports, "We have voted—all of my men will go back."

Admiral Somers leaned over the rail. "Our respects to Lord de la Warre. We, as you have heard, will return."

The sailors in the longboat broke into rousing cheers.

The leader of the longboat was looking at Somers'

tattered uniform. He was handing something over the rail, trying, from a dangerous footing, to make a salute.

"You are the Admiral, sir? May I present———"

Somers pulled Newport to the rail. "The flag should be given to this gentleman here," he said. "Captain Christopher Newport."

The longboat started back. The sails on the pinnaces were hoisted. The flag of England waved in the gentle breeze of the river.

Back to Jamestown!

Somers and Gates joined Newport by the helm. Gates murmured something about courage. Newport, nodded and smiled, but did not answer. Deep inside, though, he was thinking: If only John Smith could have seen these men today, how great would have been his pride!

Admiral Somers gazed at the banks of the wilderness land.

"There will yet be," he said to himself, "an English nation in the New World."

15

THE Indians had seen the four little pinnaces go
down the river; they wandered over the ruins of Jamestown. At last, at last, these Englishmen were gone
forever. The game would return, right into the settlement itself, sniffing the wreckage of the huts, munch-
ing the rank leafage where once the white men had
sown corn.

The red men probably feasted that day. Certainly
they rejoiced.

Then came news that the small ships had returned, with all their men. Worse news followed. Three large ships with many sails had arrived, bringing many more men. And boxes and bags and barrels—of food, of powder and bullets. Strong men these were—well fed, and full of strength. How stubborn these English were!

Again the forest rang with the sound of axes; again plows dug deep into the rich earth. They were building more cabins, rebuilding that wretched fort, mending that rotting, broken palisade.

Soon after came more ships and men, a new leader, and, very, very strange animals. On the cargo lists were, for the first time, "twelve cows—twenty goats."

The red men had never seen their like. Many were horned, like deer, but here the resemblance ended. Some were small, unruly beasts who plunged and bucked and made harsh cries. Others were big-bodied, slow-moving creatures with short legs, but they came at a man's call. Most of them gave milk. And, to the red man's amazement and horror, the white men drank it. To drink the milk of a beast! It was unthinkable. Would they not turn into beasts themselves?

The Indians watched with hopeful interest. And with alarm they watched the new leader, Sir Thomas

Dale. His first move was to see about those rather feeble forts on the jutting points of Cape Henry and Point Comfort. The forts were made larger, stronger; heavier guns appeared—more men.

Thus the dismayed Indian eyed the colony, so swiftly come to life once more.

Sir Thomas Dale is known in history as the "Iron Governor"—a most fitting name. Of iron, indeed, was his own energy, his will, and his rule. He was far too severe to be loved by the colonists. Many hated him; all were forced to respect him. It is probable that iron was needful. The colonists were coming more and more rapidly. Many were not easy to govern.

The forts settled, Dale turned to Jamestown. Nothing there suited him. The church was in need of repair. There was a new well to be dug. There must be a storehouse for ammunition, a shelter for cattle, a blockhouse westward for protection against the Indians.

Now he started new settlements: Dale's Gift, Henricus, Bermuda, Shirley's Hundreds. These were mere clusters of huts, with a landing for a boat and a palisade. There was always a palisade. Like John Smith, Dale realized the more white men the less friendly the red men.

So far, the Indians had not been openly unfriendly. They had made no attacks in force, but many hunters in the forests, many men working in outlying fields, never came home. Those new animals, too, proved a temptation. The Indian certainly desired no milk from beasts, but they might provide a new taste in meat. More and more cattle disappeared in the dark hours of the night.

None the less, the colony was growing. Those old ideas of the passage to Cathay, of gold mines to make all men rich overnight, were all but forgotten in the press of perpetual work. Both the colonists and the Company now realized that this new land had other gifts to offer. Its gifts were not so glamorous as the wealth of the Orient, or Spain's pearls and golden bars, but simpler things.

The ships going back to England were now well laden. They carried quantities of excellent lumber, pitch and tar for the British shipyards, bales of fine furs, and herbs and roots useful in medicine, especially the pungent sassafras. Now and again, there was some small measure of tobacco. England had now known tobacco for years, and despite outcries against it, there were many who liked it. The English were getting it, in slowly increasing quantities, through Spain, from the West Indies.

No one saw at this time how swiftly its use would increase, and that soon, very soon, tobacco was to become Virginia's long-sought mine of gold.

At this time every colonist worked for the Company. The fields were common fields, and in them was planted only what the colonists needed and the Company desired. Dale had a new idea, and the Company assented. Let each man have a plot of ground of his very own, on which to grow whatever he chose. Well did the Governor know the Englishman's love of land, his pride of possession.

The change was no less than a miracle. Men who had grumbled at the long hours in the common fields now doubled their efforts to get back to their own small holdings. Quarrels became less frequent, conversation turned upon plantings.

Governor Dale looked about him with satisfaction —his idea had worked. Additions and improvements were being made to the cabins—the garden plots were thriving. Making sure that no hand in Jamestown was idle, he went to inspect the new settlement of Henricus. Here he noted a singularly well kept garden, all of tobacco. The plants seemed larger. The owner straightened up from weeding a long row, and approached him. Somewhat shyly, he gave his name—John Rolfe. The Governor remembered him as one of the Bermuda men, a devout member of the church whose young wife had died in Jamestown.

Rolfe broke a tobacco leaf. He had been experimenting with the Indian weed, hoping to grow a better plant. Someday, perhaps, this Virginia tobacco might be as good as the Spanish; already he thought the leaf was larger, the fragrance improved. The Governor sniffed deeply and, smiling, commended Master Rolfe highly.

The smile changed suddenly to a scowl. A boat was about to set sail from the landing—he recognized it as Captain Argall's boat. He hastened to the dock.

Argall was Dale's right-hand man. He was tireless in exploration, in finding favorable new sites for settlements. He had protected England's interests with zeal, cruising far north to drive the French from Port Royal, from Mount Desert off the coast of Maine. He had captured Spanish spies on the Virginia coast and dragged them to Jamestown and to jail. His sharp eyes missed nothing. Dale knew Argall's value, but he neither liked nor wholly trusted him.

Where was he bound for now?

"To an Indian village," Argall replied. "They have promised many good furs."

Dale did not think this a very good time for trading; the Indians had not been friendly. It was certainly no time to give them cause for anger.

Argall nodded toward the boat. He had excellent goods for trading; and, in case of trouble, good men and plenty of ammunition.

Again Dale protested. They wished no Indian troubles now.

Argall, in turn, disliked Dale; he disliked advice even more. He made no reply. Briefly he waited to see if Dale would actually forbid him to go. Dale did not. The sails went up, and the boat departed.

16

WHEN Argall returned from the trip Governor Dale gazed at him with curiousity. He could not remember ever having seen Argall smile before.

Argall's smile broadened, not too pleasantly. He reminded the governor of his fears—that he, Argall, might cause trouble with the Indians? Instead, he had ensured peace. He had brought to Jamestown, as hostage, the beloved daughter of Powhatan, the Princess Pocahontas. She had been visiting at the village

141

of a kinsman, one Japazaws, where Argall had gone for the furs.

Japazaws, himself, had given her over but it had not been easy. At first, all bribes had been resisted. Japazaws felt his duties as both kinsman and host. Also, he probably felt a certain fear of Powhatan. But all had been overcome by a very large, highly polished copper kettle. He simply could not resist that kettle.

Argall saw no reason why the young prisoner should not wander at will. Perhaps a sentry or two at night would be enough? He was sure the Indians would not come. He was correct.

If Powhatan's fury was great, his care for the safety of Pocahontas was greater. Argall's bold stroke, though dishonorable, was successful. White hunters roamed the forest, and men worked in the fields, unharmed.

The little princess spent much time on the river bank. When a ship came, she stood a little apart, her dark eyes wide, eagerly watching each man who came ashore. But the tall Captain did not come; instead came news of him.

He had recovered from that dire wound received in Virginia. Once more he had gone, as a soldier for England, and died in a fierce sea fight off the Azores.

For days Pocahontas stayed in her cabin. Argall, puzzled, sent the few women in Jamestown to see her, but they could do nothing. She would not stir; she would not eat—she was like a ghost.

Dale, alarmed, flew into a rage with Argall. He had been a little too smart. Now, if Pocahontas died, how could they prove to Powhatan that they had had no hand in it? The Indians would descend upon them and every colonist would be murdered!

Dale, with all his cruelty, his love of power, was a godly man. He had from the first felt pity for this lonely young prisoner. When his temper had cooled, he went to see her himself.

In fatherly fashion he talked, and the girl listened, at first with vacant, dry eyes. Then, after a while, she wept.

Had Argall seen Dale at this moment, he would have been amazed.

Gently the "Iron Governor" coaxed the sobbing princess to eat a little. Through her sobs she told him she had lost a dearly beloved friend. She had overheard the news from the men on the last ship.

Dale came back next day, and for many days thereafter. His harsh voice lowered, he read her some comforting passages from the Bible. Then he spoke of that other world, that hereafter, where dear friends would meet again to walk in sunny meadows, under flowering trees. Dale suggested Pocahontas leave the darkness of her cabin and walk in the sunshine.

Like a child she obeyed.

Daughter of the great outdoors, there could be no medicine, no balm to her heart better than the sun. She was young—soon she was hungry. Her lagging footsteps grew lighter, her color came back, her eyes were bright again.

Often, when the Governor came back from some tiresome journey, or even more tiresome meeting, he would find a bunch of wild flowers in his bare little office. As long as they could be gotten, they were always violets. He had told her once they grew in England, too.

John Rolfe came up from Henricus with some new tobacco to show the Governor. The Governor was out and Rolfe waited. He was very tired; he dozed a little, and dreamed. When he awoke, he believed himself still dreaming. In the doorway stood a girl, the late sunlight gleaming gold upon her copper colored skin, burnishing her black hair. Swiftly she was gone.

So did John Rolfe first see the Princess Pocahontas.

He came to Jamestown often after that with a new

bit of tobacco, or to ask about the ships' sailings; sometimes with no excuse at all.

He joined the princess as she walked along the river or in the forest. At first she was shy and silent, then more friendly as he helped her gather flowers or berries to carry to some ill man or some young mother.

Jamestown watched with interest, Captain Argall most of all.

Suppose, he suggested to the Governor, young Master Rolfe should marry the Indian princess? Might it not bring an even more lasting peace?

The Governor was sharp. Rolfe was a pious young man; the little maid was gentle and good, but after all, she was a heathen. He had himself spoken to her on matters of religion, but she had not said much to him.

Almost on Argall's heels came John Rolfe. He twisted his hat round and round in his hands; he was slow in speaking.

He had fought himself for weeks, months. He knew the English did not as a rule marry the red folk, but Pocahontas liked the ways of the English. As for religion, she truly seemed a Christian and she was willing to be baptized.

Dale looked into the crimson face, the somber eyes.

"And," he assisted, "you are young; she is beautiful, and you are much in love."

So Pocahontas was baptized with the Biblical name of Rebecca, and soon afterward she became Rebecca Rolfe. The log church seemed more garden than church, so lavish were the flowers at this season. The church was packed, by lord and laborer alike. Powhatan did not come; he sent, in his place, his brother and two tall sons.

It is reported that Rolfe and his wife dwelt "civilly and lovingly" at the plantation at Henricus and, in due time, came a son.

At the end of two years Rolfe proposed a trip to England. He longed for a sight of his own country, deeply though he had come to love this one. Pocahontas was as eager as a child. In the long winter evenings he had told her much of his homeland.

And, as a child, she enjoyed it. Her eyes widened at sight of wide streets and fine houses, the great buildings, the rich costumes, the wonders of the theater.

Attentions were lavished on the "princess"; everywhere she was entertained. In the beginning there had been, perhaps, a measure of curiosity, but the beauty, the simple friendliness of the Indian girl charmed them all.

It is not known when or how she heard that the tall Captain was yet alive, or whether she ever saw him. There are many reports, some saying yes, some no.

All through the months in the strange land, she truly deserved her title of "princess." Dignified but gracious, she rendered shy, almost childish thanks for all hospitality, all gifts.

When spring came with its first warm winds, she turned questioning eyes upon her husband, and he answered before she had time to speak.

Yes, it was spring; they would go home. He, too, was weary of London streets; he felt an urge for their own plantation, for Virginia.

At the port of Gravesend he pointed out the ship which would take them. They would have only a few days' wait now.

That night Pocahontas seemed strangely tired; her hands and face were burning hot. Soon she was talking, sometimes to Rolfe, sometimes to herself.

The doctor came and shook his head. It was fever. The dread small-pox had broken out suddenly in the port. Hastily Rolfe sent for friends; the baby was hastily taken away.

Pocahontas woke and missed him; Rolfe soothed her. The baby would stay in the country, where there were trees and green fields, until she felt better.

Again she spoke. It would be spring now in Virginia, with the white trees and the red in great drifts against the dark forest. It had been about this time the first white winged ships had come from England. In spring she had walked along the river bank with the tall soldier.

She tried to speak. Rolfe leaned closer.

She wished they had gone home a little sooner, when the woods were blue with violets.

Rolfe rushed out into the spring rain, stumbling blindly through the streets. He found a flower seller in the shelter of an arch.

Pocahontas held the violets, cool and wet, against her blazing face, drinking in their faint woodland fragrance. She smiled. Then again she tried to speak, and Rolfe bent to catch the words.

How swiftly they had come home——

Then the violets fell from her limp hands, across her now silent heart.

THE MASSACRE

17

EVEN in the short time Rolfe had been away, Virginia had seen changes. Dale had gone to England, and the colony struggled and suffered under the rule of Captain Argall. But there were more new settlements, plantations with larger houses, ever widening fields. On his return Rolfe noted that many were planted with tobacco.

The very land rang with protests against Argall; his punishments, his taxes, his dishonesty. Soon the protests grew louder, echoing across the seas. Every ship brought letters, petitions, and shouting deputies. The Company and the King were fair deafened by the complaints. Argall was recalled. Lord de la Warre himself set forth to try to settle matters, but died on the voyage.

Both Dale and the colony had wanted George Yeardley as Governor. In April, 1619, he came back, and was met with acclaim. He had some remarkable news. No longer were the Virginia colonists to be governed by the King and Company alone; they were to have a voice in their own affairs. In addition to the Governor's Council, there was to be another one. Two representatives from each settlement were to be chosen by the people themselves. These representatives would deal with matters close at hand, such as religion, the Indian problems, agriculture.

Thus was born the House of Burgesses—that tiny seed of self-government which, in the long years to come, was destined to grow and flourish; to become, in the end, the foundation of America's freedom.

Self-government today is taken for granted; in that long-ago time it was unheard of. There was much talk and unbounded enthusiasm. Without delay representatives were elected.

In the steaming heat of late July, twenty-two Burgesses sat in the log church at Jamestown. The Governor and his Council sweltered under their robes of state, but no one seemed to mind.

There was still more news. It concerned land, that subject most dear to the colonists. Following Dale's idea of small, private plots, each colonist who had come before 1616 was to be accorded many broad acres for a very small rent. According to their means, the men paid. The wealthy acquired vast lands, thus beginning the great plantations, but the poorer, too, bought, and smaller farms came into being.

As time passed, more and more did acreage, large and small, go for the planting of tobacco. Its popularity was growing apace. Every ship carried more and more to England.

Now came another result of the Company's new ideas. Would not these Virginia men be more content if they had real home life? It seemed worth a trial.

The next ship brought a new cargo—possible wives. There were ninety women—some poor girls, some early widowed by England's wars, but all had been carefully chosen, for life in the wilderness was hard. They must be healthy and young and, the Company thoughtfully added, "handsome." Their pas-

sage money was to be paid by the eager husbands. Mostly it was paid in tobacco—a neat sum of one hundred and twenty pounds.

Wedding after wedding followed. Soon the cabins, the lonely houses of the planters, were brightened. As the Company had hoped, they were becoming "homes." Men came from toil to see blue chimney smoke rising, to smell the savory fragrance of suppers cooking, then to hear a woman's eager footsteps running to the door with a cheery voice of welcome.

Each ship was now bringing more colonists, but still the widening fields needed more labor—there was never enough. The last ships brought a new type of labor—the indentured men. Some were merely too poor to pay their passage. They would, for its payment, serve a master for a term of years. These men were quickly taken over by the planters, but still more were wanted.

Then came the practice of sending beggers from the streets of the seaports and prisoners from the jails. Some of the prisoners were only unfortunate men jailed for debts they could not pay or for holding religious and political views differing from those then in power. Unfortunately, there were among them real criminals, thieves and murderers.

It must have been difficult for the planters to select when they looked the men over, but there was labor to be done and all were taken.

In this same year came a Dutch ship up the river, with more labor for sale—Negroes taken on the coast of Africa. There were only twenty, and the prices were high, but they too were taken.

Now the fields widened still more, and the houses were enlarged for growing families. Already the pattern of the plantation was set: the "big house" of the planter, the small cabins for the laborers, the great barns, the many small buildings, dairy and smokehouse and workshop.

Occasionally, a few Indians drifted into the settlements with venison and wild turkey and a few furs to trade, but their comings were not frequent. The forest lay singularly silent—too silent. Had John Smith been in Virginia he would have noted this silence months past. He would have made some excuse to wander on the trails, to stop at some of the Indian villages. He would have seen—and known.

Shadowy figures were constantly on the move among the trees, going from tribe to tribe with messages. Night after night councils were held around the campfires. There were angry speeches and plans.

Tribes hitherto foes to one another were friendly. There was but one foe now—the white man.

The spring of 1622 came early, and the white men went joyfully about their planting of wheat, corn, flax, and tobacco. The cattle, released from their winter barns, grazed happily in the flower-starred meadows. Fifteen years ago, in such a spring, those first English ships had come sailing up the river. As the Virginians worked, they paused now and again to look about them. It was, truly, a lovely land.

Then one day a sentry on the fort at Jamestown saw, far off down the river, a column of smoke. This was no chimney smoke, but a fire. Now it was boiling up in black, angry clouds. The sentry turned to shout to his fellow sentries, but they were shouting too.

One pointed to smoke up the river, another to boats overladen with women and children. The men at the oars were rowing like madmen. The sentries did not wait to find out the trouble. Their trumpets sounded a loud, long alarm as men were seen running from the far fields.

Now the boats were at the landing, and people came tumbling in. Sobbing women, wailing children, men ashen gray under their heavy tan, all had the one cry—Indians!

Nothing was very clear. Breathless, exhausted hunters had come to their settlement, telling them to flee. It was hoped to warn a few more places near by, but already whole settlements had been set on fire and the people killed.

Swiftly men strove to close the heavy gates of the Jamestown palisade.

Jamestown and the people who had gained that refuge were saved, but the outlying hamlets and plantations were destroyed. Smoke, blinding, choking, hung heavy on the air. Everywhere it was the same grim story—smoking ruins, the pitiful bodies of men, women and children brutally slain. The red men had, in one day, come in force by hundreds, perhaps thousands; it had seemed millions.

Slowly the dead were counted—three hundred and forty-seven.

Swiftly, companies were organized to follow those red men. And for many weeks they did—destroying Indian villages, slaughtering without mercy men, women and children, driving them farther and farther westward.

No longer would the colonists trust the red neighbors. They were ever ready, ever watchful.

Had this appalling massacre come sooner, the colony might again have been abandoned.

But to many, especially the younger English, this land was home, and these fields in which they had labored and fought were their own. Slowly the charred earth was ploughed again and the houses rebuilt.

The Indians marveled.

How stubborn these white men were!

18

ALTHOUGH the Indians had been driven westward, the next years saw the English pushing farther westward, also. More and more colonists were pouring in; more and more plantations and farms arose farther up the rivers. There was no open warfare, but all too frequently these lonely settlements were attacked by small parties of wandering red men.

The House of Burgesses met and decided to build a long palisade. Well fortified, and well manned, it

161

would stretch across the northern part of the peninsula, to protect the settlers on the James and York Rivers.

It was called Middle Plantation, and it was soon surrounded by new settlements—a scattering of houses near the palisade, and outlying farms and plantations.

It was far from a real town at that time, yet it was destined to become the capital of all Virginia—Williamsburg.

But even as the Virginians were watching the Indians as they went westward, they were also turning their attention eastward—to old England. Eagerly, but sometimes, fearfully, they listened to the news the ships were bringing.

In the year 1624 King James had coldly refused to give a new charter to the Virginia Company. Hereafter, he decreed, the Crown would send out the governors. The Virginia men were alarmed. Would that mean their treasured House of Burgesses would be abolished? Everyone knew King James disliked it because its members were far too independent, to his way of thinking.

Then had come the news of James's death and that his son, Charles the First, had succeeded him. If possible, Charles detested the idea of the House of Burgesses even more than had his father. He had no taste for this new, this coming democracy.

He and his chosen deputies would rule Virginia.

Fortunately the first governors were liked. All of them—Sir Francis Wyatt, Sir George Yeardley, and Francis West—understood the problems of the colony. The House of Burgesses was scarcely missed.

Then came trouble in the form of a new governor, Doctor John Pott. To the weary ears of the King came the report that Doctor Pott was most unwelcome to the colonists. He was given to "strong waters and low company" and the even worse offense of stealing cattle.

King Charles removed Doctor Pott without delay and, in addition, sent a friendly letter concerning the House of Burgesses—and tobacco. Would not the House of Burgesses resume their meetings, long forbidden? The Virginians were delighted, until they considered the price for that privilege—the new arrangement on tobacco.

England would continue to ban Spanish tobacco in favor of that grown by the colonists, but the Mother Country would only take the amount she felt could be sold at a profit. England, of course, would decide on the price, the customs duties, and the share of profit due to the Crown!

The Burgesses met and in full agreement prepared an answer to King Charles. It is described as a "Humble Answere," but it was, none the less, a firm "No."

The House of Burgesses continued to meet. The colonists had ever treasured this small beginning of independence. There were many local problems which could scarcely wait for English decisions, and now there was a definite need for the colonists to stand together. For Charles had sent out his new governor, Sir John Harvey.

For five unpleasant years the colony endured Sir John Harvey. Then, without thanks, he was returned to England. Stubbornly the King sent him back, but shortly thereafter he was replaced by the popular Sir Francis Wyatt.

In turn, Wyatt was replaced by Sir William Berkeley. It was now thirty-five years since the first landing at Jamestown, and the colony had come a long way.

The new governor thought well of this Virginia. The plantation houses were simple, but comfortable. For mile after mile stretched the ever-widening fields with their abundant crops. Livestock throve. Food was abundant.

There was, however, one thing the governor did not like—the House of Burgesses. An aristocrat by birth, he believed strongly in royal and aristocratic rule. Here in Virginia, both aristocrats and commoners, even men of no property, had a voice in the voting. It was a trend of the times, this democracy. Even before he had left England there were open mutterings against the high-handed rule of King Charles.

The mutterings soon grew into open rebellion. At the head of the rebels against the Crown marched stern Oliver Cromwell.

For seven years the civil war raged in England, and the Virginia colony eagerly awaited each incoming ship for news.

There were a few in Virginia who favored Cromwell, but most of the colonists were intensely loyal to the King.

The final news, in 1649, shocked them. Not only had the King's forces been completely defeated, but Charles the First had been beheaded as well. Cromwell ruled all of England, and young Prince Charles had fled to safety in Europe.

Berkeley, with the consent of the House of Burgesses, invited the Prince to come to Virginia. Charles did not come. He was sure he could, in time, regain the throne of England.

However, on every incoming ship came the Royalists who had stood by the King. They not only hated Cromwell, many feared for their lives. They brought their families, their servants, what money and possessions they had managed to save.

History calls these Royalists the "Cavaliers." They were richly dressed, and they wore their hair, or wigs, in long, elaborate curls.

Cromwell's men dressed simply, as befitted these stern foes of the over-luxurious English court. They wore their hair short. Scornfully the Cavaliers called them "Roundheads."

Virginia welcomed the Cavaliers with warmth. And their coming marked a turning point in Virginia. For some years the most prosperous of the colonists had been ordering fine clothes and other luxuries from England. But most of the colonists were not wealthy enough to be able to do this. Also, for forty years they had been too busy ploughing fields and combatting the resentful red men.

Now, with the Indians more or less driven back, with the vast fields cleared and planted, with more labor to be had, the time was ripe to go further toward their final goal. That goal was: to make their simple dwellings more like those of England; to adorn them with fine pieces of furniture; to surround them with gardens. The colonists wanted also to improve their livestock; to have better herds; and to have finer horses.

The sight of the rich Cavaliers, with their talk of England, made the planters even more eager for luxuries.

The change could first be seen in the unloading of the ships.

The sailors laughed and shouted and made guesses as to the contents of the boxes.

"How light! No bullets in these! Indeed, no! They contain fine bonnets fresh from London Town, and laces and linens and fine silks! Look at the labels! And these crates are to be handled with care, for they hold violins and gilded harps for the making of music!"

Some of the cargoes were troublesome. There were crates of glossy, greedy pigeons to be fed all the way across, and even peacocks, whose outcry would wake the most weary sailorman. Fine horses crossed the Atlantic, too, and boxes filled with slips and cuttings of flowers, fruits, and vines from the Mother Country.

But soon, around the evergrowing plantations, were orchards and vineyards and gardens.

Every ship went back to England with tobacco; little else was sent now.

Then came alarm. Cromwell had heard of the Virginia offer to Prince Charles; his ships now lay off Point Comfort. Berkeley was obliged to admit that as Cromwell now ruled England, he could hardly have a royal colony across the sea, nor a royal governor.

So Berkeley resigned, and retired to his country place across the bay at Accomac. Peacefully, three governors ruled for Cromwell during the eleven years of the Commonwealth.

Virginia turned again to her wide fields and her new settlements.

Middle Plantation was growing from a mere garrison into the beginnings of a town. It became a center for the meeting of many planters, for it was more convenient than Jamestown.

Over at Accomac, Berkeley doubtless raged, as did his friends. Imagine! Roundheads were ruling Virginia!

Then in 1660 came a ship with much news: Cromwell was dead, Prince Charles was now King, and Berkeley would again be the royal Governor.

The majority rejoiced; some of the Cromwell men did not. Very soon no one was rejoicing, for Charles the Second had shown small gratitude to the loyal colony of Virginia. He had presented it to two of his favorite courtiers, Lord Culpeper and the Earl of Arlington!

They were not to "disturb" the present colonists. Nevertheless, the colonists' hearts ached. This land, for which they had suffered and toiled so long, was to be given away to newcomers—strangers!

Violent protests were sent on the next ship. They were ignored.

There was also more trouble at home. Berkeley, long deprived of power, was determined to make up for the loss. He imposed new and higher taxes. He managed to get more and more men of his own mind into the House of Burgesses. Then, having got them in, he refused for fifteen years to have new elections. There was much discontent.

To add to the colony's troubles, the outlying settlements were now being harassed by the Indians; Berkeley, despite repeated requests, refused to send the militia against them. Rumors arose that Berkeley was fattening an already fat purse by a most profitable trade with the red men for fine beaver skins.

The discontent grew, flared into anger, verged on rebellion.

In 1676 rebellion came.

19

AT JAMESTOWN sat the Council and the House of Burgesses. Most of the Burgesses were now Berkeley's chosen men, wealthy owners of large tracts of land. Some had been in office for as long as fifteen years in succession.

But on the Governor's Council sat a young man whom Berkeley hated and feared—Nathaniel Bacon. Like Berkeley he was an aristocrat; he owned a

171

plantation of some size near the Falls of the Farre West. But he was of a new generation, and he had new ideas.

Bitterly he fought each new tax on the small farmer. Why should the House of Burgesses be controlled by the large landholder? Why was there not an equal vote for the man of a few acres or of none? All had bent their backs in toil for the making of this Virginia. And why should not all have the protection of military aid against the Indians? Many men, due to the vast holdings along the shores, had been forced to take up land farther westward.

Berkeley was furious, but he promised to take up the question of the Indians at the next meeting in March. It was now winter.

Bacon was again on his feet. He cried:

"March! And until March let these murders, these burnings, go on?"

Nevertheless, the Governor would not, at this time, call out troops.

Bacon returned home to find his trusted overseer and several of his servants dead in the fields by Indian arrows. He was about to go back to Jamestown when the sound of galloping sent him swiftly to the door.

Men on lathered horses were coming into the dooryard. There were dozens of them, with fresh tales of Indian attacks. The talk grew into an uproar as more horsemen thundered in.

"Berkeley," came a shout, "is safe and snug at Jamestown—he does not know!"

"Or care!" yelled a dozen voices. The uproar became greater. "We cannot wait until March—the Indians are here now!" Would Bacon be their officer? Several hundred men could be gathered in a matter of hours.

Hastily Bacon sent a message to Jamestown to ask for orders to march against the Indians—conditions were far worse than the Governor realized.

The messenger came back—the Governor saw no reason for such undue haste or for such an order. Bacon sent more messages. By dawn men had gathered, grim and determined. More came in.

Bacon spoke. He had, he said, no order from the Governor and they might all be hanged for disobedience. Would they still care to ride against the Indians? They would.

The only real battle with the red men was brief, and easily won. The red man had courage, but more and more he was retreating westward. There still remained enough to attack, in small numbers, the lonely farms.

To Governor Berkeley came news of this march of Bacon and his men.

He was purple with rage. Bacon had defied him— he had defied the very government of England. In person Berkeley set out against these "rebels."

But a messenger overtook him on the way to say there was growing trouble at Jamestown. Many men were agreeing with Bacon. In addition, there was renewed complaint about taxes, and about new elections in the House of Burgesses. A feeling was rising that Berkeley's chosen men had held office too long. That rumor persisted about the trade in beaver skins.

Hastily, Berkeley came back to Jamestown and promised fewer and lower taxes. It was hard, at this moment, to tell friend from foe.

Then came Bacon and his men to Jamestown. The Governor had him arrested as a "rebel" but he dared go no further. Bacon's popularity was increasing by the day.

If, said the old Governor, young Bacon would apologize, and promise greater obedience in the future, he might again take his seat in the Council. Many were amazed at the strange generosity of Berkeley—perhaps Bacon most of all. For reasons of his own, especially because he wanted that promised order to fight the Indians, he rendered humble apology. There seemed to be peace, but it was an uneasy peace. Day after day, week after week, the order was delayed. The Indians continued to attack the far plantations, the lonely cabins.

The Burgesses met and quickly noted that Bacon was not in his seat with the Council. Some voice among the Burgesses announced that he had gone to see his ill wife.

The Governor scowled as he rose to open the meeting. His voice was drowned by a hubbub outside. Shouts, cheers and the increasing thunder of horses' hoofs were coming nearer and nearer. It sounded like an army! It was.

Bacon and six hundred men surged into Jamestown. Bacon, with armed guards, was at the door. Whatever Berkeley's faults were, he was not a coward. Unarmed, he came to the door and invited Bacon, if he chose, to shoot him. Bacon did not choose to do so. He merely wanted that promised order. A roar went up from his followers. They would have that order and have it now.

Berkeley gave in.

Bacon rode off with a hastily signed order and the resounding title of General and Commander-in-Chief of Indian Warfare.

With Bacon safely upcountry, the Governor again

took a high hand. He declared Bacon and his men "traitors"; he wrote to King Charles.

Then some whisper made the Governor believe his own life in danger; he left suddenly, sailing back to Accomac, with a group of his followers.

The news reached Bacon at Middle Plantation. He found it crowded with angry men. It was rumored that Berkeley had sent to England for two thousand "Red Coates" to attack Bacon—to put down what he called this "rebellion."

Bacon spoke. "How many will stand against the 'Red Coates'—even against the king?" He drew up a paper for signing.

Some hesitated.

Then came news of an Indian attack on a York River fort. Only recently the Governor had seen fit to remove all arms from that fort. It was too much. The paper was hastily signed.

Call it war, call it rebellion, call it anything you like. First, they would capture the Governor.

However, while Bacon and his troops had been battling the Indians, the sly old Governor had gathered more men to his side. The ship and its two hundred and fifty men sent to Accomac to make the capture was, instead, captured by Berkeley. The commander, Giles Bland, was put in irons and one of his officers promptly hanged.

Berkeley and his men boarded the ship; others clambered into small sloops. They set sail for Jamestown.

There were not enough men at Jamestown to resist, so they hastily departed to join with Bacon's forces up the river.

Into an almost deserted town came the triumphant Governor. Instantly fortifications with heavy cannon were set up on the narrowest part of the peninsula. Now let Mr. Bacon come! They had not long to wait.

Many more men had joined him.

Next day came battle, brief but furious. Bacon's troops, hardened from Indian fighting, were better fighters. And, too, they fought with desperation, knowing that if Berkeley were the victor, they would receive no mercy.

Amid a rain of bullets and cannon fire, Berkeley and his followers hastily set sail for Accomac.

In a rage, Bacon set fire to Jamestown, so that, as he said, "it should harbor no more rogues."

During the siege he had often staggered from fever; now he could fight no longer. In a few days he was dead.

With his death, his army fell apart, and the men drifted back to their homes.

In a few months Berkeley came back to a rebuilt Jamestown. He was an old man now, but his fury was great. He managed to capture some of the best known of the rebels. At least thirty he hanged as "traitors." Right and left he took the rebels' lands and other property.

Now, at last, Charles had gotten around to sending not only the "Red Coates," but a committee to look into this trouble in Virginia. To Berkeley's seething indignation, the committee did not share his views on punishing the rebels. The committee was sure King Charles would prefer pardons and peace. The reports on Berkeley angered Charles; he promptly recalled the old governor, and refused to hear or even see him.

New royal governors came and went, and much that Bacon had gained was again lost. The House of Burgesses was to meet only every two years, and no member was to be elected who was not a landowner. However, that fight for greater freedom was not in vain. Years later, like echoes of Bacon's ringing voice, there came others ringing out in the House of Burgesses.

Time and again there had been talk of removing the seat of government to Middle Plantation. It was more centrally located for most of the settlements; it was more protected from enemies coming from overseas; it was decidedly more healthy. In spite of all the talk, nothing was done until, by some mischance, Jamestown burned again. The government was forced to move to Middle Plantation and, after some discussion, agreed to remain there.

William and Mary now ruled England, and the new capital town was renamed, in 1698, in honor of the King, Williamsburg.

It was never to be a large town, for though some of the planters built town houses, most of these Virginia folk preferred their own plantations.

Careful planning made Williamsburg beautiful. Already the College of William and Mary had been built; from it ran Duke of Gloucester Street, a mile in length. At the far end of the street was erected the finely built brick Capitol. Beyond a long green rose the Governor's Palace, with its acres of formal gardens and its orchards. A good church was built, Bruton Parish. Shops were set up; there were taverns and inns serving fine food.

It became the meeting place for all Virginia. When the House of Burgesses met, the streets were crowded; there were also court days, auctions, days when the ships came bringing goods from England. Soon there were parties and balls.

From the plantations rolled fine coaches; from farms came sturdy carts and ox-drawn wagons. The womenfolk came with the men—to see friends, long missed, and to shop.

Trails had widened into roads, but the roads were still wretched. Every wheel was coated with the heavy, clinging red mud. There were breakdowns and delays. However, a fine coach would stop to help a heavy cart bogged down, an oxcart pause to render aid to a floundering coach. A squire of a thousand acres would hail a farmer of a few, to inquire how grew his tobacco.

A measure of democracy had been born in the early days, when titled gentleman and sturdy laborer fought, side by side, fever and famine and Indian foe. Now, as they struggled together against the mud, it continued. For that mud was a symbol—in it lay history. It was part of the soil for which all of them had toiled and fought—it was the land of Virginia.

JAMESTOWN

20

MANY years ago, waters slowly destroyed that land which was the neck of the peninsula where, behind their barricades, Bacon and Berkeley and their men fought so desperately for the possession of Jamestown. It is no longer a peninsula but Jamestown Island, a place apart.

Also, the deep river lapped steadily at the banks, slowly eating away the soil where once stood many of the cabins of the early colonists. Today a long sea wall keeps the river back.

The roofless church tower still stands, its burns and scars hidden by a thick cloak of ivy. The church has been restored to shelter the worn gravestones in the chancel. Outside is the graveyard, with its ancient gnarled trees, its old, old stones, mossgrown and broken.

Here folk tread softly, reverently, and speak in low tones, as if fearful of disturbing these brave dead.

To many, Jamestown is a lonely, a tragic place, to others a place of peace. Truly, this little island saw ruin, despair and death. But now the evil days are long gone and the hard struggle long over. Here was born England in the new world, to become, in time, the United States of America.

A national monument now towers, gleaming white, strong and simple, against the blue Virginia sky.

Outside the churchyard stands a statue of Pocahontas clad, Indian fashion, in a fringed dress of buckskin, her long hair falling about her serious young face. She seems about to step from her stone pedestal, to walk again in the dim paths among the trees; to wander again in the sunny meadows, gold with buttercups, purple with wild violets.

Close to the river bank stands another statue—that of Captain John Smith.

Beside it towers a pine, strangely like Smith himself—tall, straight, but weather-beaten by many storms.

There is little else actually to see at Jamestown, but even to walk upon that ground brings to the mind thoughts of its courageous history. To stand by the bank is to see the first white-sailed ships coming slowly up the wide river. To wander on the little paths among the whispering trees is to see the shadowy forms of the Indians, slipping silently through the forest. To step in that quiet church is to join in the gaiety of long-ago weddings and christenings, to share in the sorrow of the many burials. It is to see the solemn Burgesses at their early meetings, awed but grateful for their first small taste of freedom.

And—now—once more to look at the figures of the sturdy Captain and the slim Indian maid—to dream anew of that great love whose memory has endured for centuries in the minds and hearts of men.

6310